THE BEAST OF JERSEY

The
Beast of Jersey

by
his wife, Joan Paisnel

NEW ENGLISH LIBRARY
TIMES MIRROR

First published in Great Britain by Robert Hale & Co., 1972
© Max Caulfield and European Press Enterprises, 1972

*

FIRST NEL PAPERBACK EDITION SEPTEMBER 1973
Reissued in this new edition March 1975

*

NEL Books are published by
New English Library Limited from Barnard's Inn, Holborn, London E.C.1.
Made and printed in Great Britain by Hunt Barnard Printing Ltd., Aylesbury, Bucks.

45002624 8

CONTENTS

ACKNOWLEDGEMENTS

I would like to express my sincere thanks to the many people who assisted me towards achieving the publication of this book. In particular I would like to record my special thanks to Max Caulfield who advised me as to the writing of the manuscript and carried the main burden of editing the material; to Alan Shadrake and John Lisners, two Fleet Street journalists who are largely responsible for the extensive research involved and to James Nicholson also of Fleet Street who rendered us all invaluable assistance on certain key points.

JOAN PAISNEL

ONE

MIDNIGHT CAR CHASE

Less than three miles from the farmhouse where I live on Jersey lies La Nez point from which, on anything but the worst of days, the coast of France is clearly visible. What is really notable about it, however, is not the vista, for even better views can be obtained farther east, but a huge granite rock, over forty feet high, called Rocqueberg.

Even today, a clammy sense of evil broods about this place. Centuries ago, the top of the rock was vitrified by lightning and on a ledge half-way down there are strange indentations like the hoof-marks of a goat or other horned animal. Once, the witches of Jersey, who had dedicated their lives to the Devil, met here to celebrate their satanic orgies. A handful of these practitioners of the Black Arts were caught. In 1585, one Jean Mourant of the parish of St Clement, was sentenced to be strangled and then burned, the court declaring, 'Having been so forgetful of his salvation as to make a convenant with Satan, he confessed with his own mouth his dealings with the Devil by mark and pact, confirmed by the gift of one of his members, by means of which he had committed infinite mischiefs, crimes and homicides.' The 'gift' in his case was his finger-joint which he had cut off as a sacrifice to his Dark Master. It was his method of inflicting the notorious *merche du diable* upon his body, for all witches were under compulsion to mark their flesh in some indelible way.

Twenty-six years after Mourant had suffered his horrible fate, three women who had taken part in sabbat orgies upon the blasted rock were also legally strangled and burned. Yet another met the same fate in the Royal Square of St Helier in 1648, a contemporary writer recording, 'Such crowds came to watch her execution that the Town was full.'

This handful were among the unfortunate few who, at one time or another have been punished for witchcraft in Jersey. Most of the Devil-worshippers of Rocqueberg, in fact, were never discovered and continued to go about their daily lives without even being suspected. Today, the site of their black rituals stands in what is part of a private garden and orgies no longer disturb the serenity of this particular bit of the coastal scene. Summer visitors, no doubt, may sometimes indulge themselves with macabre thoughts at the site, at the same time presumably comforting themselves with the idea that these old superstitions are dead now. The more sensational British newspapers often carry long articles about witchcraft, certainly, but few rational people believe that such goings-on are anything more than a fashionable way of dressing up a sex orgy. The idea that people believe in a real Devil or Horned God and worship him as the embodiment of Evil seems too fantastic.

Yet witches and warlocks do exist; and there are people who do worship Satan. And Jersey, in particular, remains an island full of strange superstitions. Evil, which many people tend to regard as just another superstition that can be easily dispelled by the magic wand of the doctor, psychiatrist, scientist or revolutionary, also is a real force which can influence our lives as much as food, drink, drug-addiction or television.

For most people, luckily, these dark practices are something they simply read about. They may scan them leisurely in the newspapers with vicarious relish, safe in the knowledge that they are never likely to meet a Black Magician or experience at firsthand the evil that they deliberately create.

It was otherwise with me. For thirteen years I was married to and lived alongside a man who, unknown to me, not only practised the Black Arts but created a reign of terror in the lovely island where I live with a series of the most terrible assaults and sex crimes on women and little children, both boys and girls. A man who came increasingly to identify himself and his actions with one of the most infamous mass-murderers in history, Gilles de Rais, Marshal of France and champion of St Joan of Arc and the original Bluebeard who is credited with having killed more than 300 children to satisfy his carnal lusts and as a sacrifice to those black powers which he hoped would reward him with untold wealth. I was – and, indeed, still am – married to Edward John Louis ('Ted') Paisnel, the sex-fiend now known as the Beast of Jersey, who is serving a thirty year sentence for his crimes; who told the police when they arrested him, 'Two hundred years ago, they'd have burned me for this.'

On the night of 10th July 1971, PCs John Riseborough and Tom McGinn of the Jersey States police were driving slowly around the streets of St Helier, the capital of Jersey, in their patrol car, keeping a wary eye open for the kind of trouble that can afflict a holiday town that suffers an annual influx of half-a-million summer visitors. Although Jersey has recently become an international centre for big-time criminals, engaged in smuggling, drugs-running and crime of every description, Riseborough and McGinn had no thought of a big capture in mind. What they were on the look-out for was the odd punch-up in a pub or the drunken motorist who had got the idea that the back streets of St Helier had suddenly become the race-track at Brands Hatch.

At about 11.45 on the Route du Fort, not far from the sea-front, the police car idled up to a set of traffic lights and stopped, facing east. A long coach, full of holidaymakers on a mystery tour, pulled up alongside them and waited for the red to change. At that moment, a small Morris 1100 saloon which had driven up on the far side of the coach took it into his head to jump the lights. Riseborough and McGinn exchanged glances; it is not all that often a police car is in the lucky position of being able to catch a culprit red-handed.

Neither, it ought to be emphasized, at this stage had any other idea than to stop the miscreant and proffer him a stern reprimand. The small force of 135 regular, professional police on the island have generally more than enough on their hands during the summer months just keeping order than to waste their time 'booking' every motorist who, technically, breaks the law.

PC McGinn pressed the accelerator and the patrol car, taking the matter a trifle nonchalantly, eased after the small saloon. It never entered the head of either officer that they were going to have any difficulty nailing their quarry. Within a second or so they would accelerate alongside and Riseborough would wave the man down. However, before they could pull up alongside, the Morris had turned right into Cleveland Road, leading to the seafront at Havre des Pas. It appeared to be accelerating and Riseborough and McGinn thought it was time the driver realized the police were after him. So Riseborough turned on the blue flashing light on the car roof and McGinn flashed his head-lights.

The Morris simply ignored them. McGinn braced himself, gripping the steering wheel a little tighter and putting his foot down a little more firmly. What was the idiot up to ? Why didn't he halt ?

At the end of Cleveland Road, the Morris ought to have stopped at a yellow line to give way to any traffic along the Havre des Pas. Instead, it careered round the corner on to the main road as though driven by Steve McQueen in the film 'Bullitt'. As it darted along Havre des Pas, it swept over the white line marking the centre of the road and sideswiped an oncoming car. Yet it still did not stop. McGinn decided that just in case their quarry had *not* looked in his mirror and thought the flashing headlights simply meant that another larky driver was following, now activated his police klaxon. It had no more effect than the flashing headlights or the blue flasher on the roof. Instead, the driver of the 1100 pressed on even harder, despite the fact that both policemen could see that he was 'a pretty rotten driver'.

The Morris now crossed another yellow line which was an obligatory stop and turned right towards Grève d'Azette, still hugging the coastline. By this time, both Riseborough and McGinn sensed that they were on to something a little more important than the ordinary drunk. After all, on an island as small as Jersey, only nine miles long by five wide, opportunities to shake off a determined police pursuit are limited. Not that the lone figure they could see at the wheel of the Morris seemed to be in the least worried by this. Riseborough and McGinn felt that this might be just important enough to let H.Q. know, so Riseborough contacted Police Headquarters in Rouge Bouillon on his radio-telephone, informing them that they had taken up a chase and were at that moment at The Dicq.

He had scarcely given this information when the 1100 swerved left and careered round a blind corner with such a disregard for the niceties of driving conduct, or even elementary skill, that it went way over a white line again and continued for a short distance on the wrong side of the road before finally getting into the right lane. A short distance along this road and the 1100 driver found himself about to climb up the exhaust pipe of a car ahead of him which had slowed down to take a corner left. Instead of braking, he simply swung out to his wrong side again. Once again, he somehow got his wraggling car under control and got back on his right side before taking a chance and swerving out on to the main St Clement's Inner Road. A little way along here and the Morris faced another set of traffic lights, again set red. Without a second's hesitation, he went clean through, luckily without hitting anything. Klaxon roaring, Riseborough and McGinn followed, McGinn just having time to check his speedometer and note that they had topped the 50 mph mark. On the long straight road ahead, the speed now increased markedly and the needle soared to 70 mph. The Morris was bucking and swaying from side to side in a way that usually indicates an inexperienced driver, stretched well beyond his limit.

'It's a stolen job' murmured Riseborough and McGinn nodded.

The chase continued along Green Road, along St Clement's Hill Road and towards La Blinerie Lane. The erratic driving gave the police no chance to catch up and force their quarry to stop. Riseborough had had twelve years experience in police cars but, as he told the Royal Court of Jersey later, 'this was the worst case I have been ever involved in'. Both he and McGinn were now more worried that an innocent pedestrian or other car driver might be killed than anything else and did not try to push their man beyond a top speed of 75 mph.

Even so, this seemed to be beyond the powers of the figure crouched over the wheel of the Morris 1100. Even as Riseborough gave H.Q. another fix and requested help, both policemen were now certain that they were dealing with a Jerseyman and probably a farmer from the eastern end of the island at that, for obviously he knew the local roads like the back of his hand. No visitor, however skilful a driver, could have manipulated the corners and gradients and roads in this fashion. Even so, at the corner of La Blinerie and Samarès Lanes, he suddenly appeared to overreach himself. At the bend just before the junction, the 1100 appeared to go temporarily out of control. Yet somehow the driver got himself round left into La Blinerie Lane before making a James Bond effort to shake the police by turning right into a private lane. In fact, he was not James Bond and he had misjudged his turning, for he found himself in a blind alley. He had, it was later discovered intended to take the *next* right turn which would, indeed, have given him a clear road.

As it was, however, he darted into the private turning, catching part of the wooden fence on the offside – the wood came away and fell just in time to catch the police car with a terrible clunk. Both cars were still travelling at what by any standards was an excessive speed but nothing short of an atomic bomb would have now shaken off the police pursuit. Lacking such a persuasive armoury, the 1100 driver nevertheless showed a considerable degree of determination. The lane quickly petered out in a heavy wooden gate barring the way to a private footpath across a garden.

Without a second's hesitation, the 1100 driver went through this gate and careered along the footpath, followed rather blindly by the slightly bewildered police. For once, the quarry evinced the kind of skill that in other circumstances might have gained him a job as a stunt driver for the films. As he tore up the footpath and started across the garden, he faced the perils of a cesspit. But with all the panache of a McQueen or Connery at their most outrageous, he appeared literally to hoist the 1100 across it as though he were jumping a horse. Straight in front of him rose a bank and hedge almost eight feet high, leading to a tomato field. Without, apparently, easing the accelerator for a single second, he drove the small saloon through the hedge, tearing an immense hole in it. McGinn and Riseborough just had time to see him go through the hedge like one of Eisenhower's tanks during the U.S. break-out of the Normandy *bocage* during the Second World War when they suddenly found themselves in the trap that had been neatly set for them. With an odd, buckling, grinding cluck, their car came to rest in the cesspit.

McGinn found that he could not open his offside door but Riseborough, a rugby-player, was able to get out and he quickly flung himself across the small garden towards the gap in the hedge. At this stage, he felt that they had probably lost their man. But as he got to the impromptu opening, he saw that they had had an amazing stroke of luck. The Morris, which had made a brave, if forlorn attempt to cut a swathe across the tomato field had stopped (later it was discovered that two of the bamboo canes supporting the tomato plants had rammed through the front of the radiator grille and stopped the engine). Riseborough could just see a small, stocky figure clumping its way desperately among the tomato crop. At once, he gave chase; in other circumstances, the scene might have had a touch of farce about it. The chase continued for about 200 yards through the thicket of tomato plants, bamboo canes and soft yielding earth until the quarry reached the main road again, hotly pursued by Riseborough. Tom McGinn, meanwhile, had radioed a fix of their position to H.Q. and was told that another police car was on its way to help.

Once he clumped out on the road, Riseborough's athletic prowess soon paid off and he quickly began to overhaul the desperately fleeing figure in front of him. Then, in a superbly low (fortunately for him) tackle, he brought his man down. It was as though he had tackled a wildcat, however. Despite his superior height and weight, the burly policeman found it any-

12

thing but easy to subdue his man who fought back with demonical fury.

The man was not only strong and desperate, but cunning. As they wrestled together, he suddenly pleaded, 'I've got a bad heart'. For a brief moment, Riseborough relaxed slightly before he recalled that this was an old trick. The arrival of McGinn and reinforcements in another patrol car quickly put an end to any further efforts of the man to escape. He was bundled into the second police car and driven rapidly to Police Headquarters.

In the light of what they were to discover in the ground floor interview room in the Rouge Bouillon, both Riseborough and McGinn now tend to laugh at their initial attitude towards their captive. At this stage they had no idea that they were dealing with anything other than a simple case of taking and driving away a motor-car without the consent of the owner and with dangerous and reckless driving (in due course, the man would be charged with seven motoring offences). Both men set about dressing down the man, emphasizing what seemed to them the most heinous aspect of the crime – the wrecking of their patrol car.

'It looks like a write-off,' McGinn warned the prisoner, 'You're in for it.'

It was not until they got him into H.Q. and had a proper look that the policemen began to realize that they had stumbled across something a lot more significant than they had ever dreamed of. Their prisoner turned out to be a thick-set man of about five feet six inches, with a ginger moustache and receding hair combed back sharply from his forehead in the style still usual among the middle-aged. He was in his mid-forties (in fact, he gave his age as 46) and he had curious, deep-set, burning eyes. However, it was neither the face nor figure that held the police attention. What was startling about this man was that he was wearing a blue coat from each of whose shoulders projected a row of very sharp nails, each one-inch long and with the sharp end outwards and there were further nails sewn in similar fashion on the inside of his left lapel. Riseborough rather ruefully realized that if he had attempted to apprehend the man in the usual way by placing his hands on his shoulders or had even attempted to grab his left lapel, then he would have been in for a painful shock. Furthermore, around his wrists, the man had fixed two cloth bands, one black, the other white, each also studded with projecting nails.

A policeman, attempting to capture this man in any of the more usual ways, would not only have found it impossible to hold him but might have been disabled sufficiently to give up any pursuit. Only Riseborough's rugby training and his decision to tackle low, indeed, had done the trick. The big policeman looked at the prisoner with a new interest. This, clearly, was an unusual customer. Riseborough could not recall that at any time, in the annals of police history, had a man armed himself so thoroughly, short of carrying firearms, to evade capture.

A thorough and unusual careful police scrutiny followed. The khaki-coloured sports shirt and the pair of grey trousers the prisoner was wearing were in no way odd or unusual. What was more than a little queer, however, was that the man was wearing *carpet slippers*. The pair of woollen gloves he was wearing might or might not be innocent – certainly it was an unusual time of the year to be wearing gloves at all, a hot night in July. It would appear, in fact, that they were being worn in order to ensure that no fingerprints were left in some, presumably, compromising situation. And there was something almost *outrè* about the belt with a home-made sheath. Now exactly what was that sheath for?

The police now turned their attention to the contents of the blue coat. These proved to be even more mysterious and fascinating. First, out came an extraordinary wig with stiff, spiky *black* hair. Then a small silver torch covered with black tape to cut down the spread of light. In addition, there were two lengths of what appeared to be sashcord, a pyjama cord, a woollen cap, a handkerchief, a watch, several empty cigarette packets as well as a black cotton glove. Why should a man hoard lengths of sashcord? Why carry a pyjama cord; why *empty* cigarette packets? What was the purpose of a *single* black cotton glove?

'We'd better get the C.I.D. in on this,' said Riseborough.

The police had brought the man into H.Q. at approximately 12.10 a.m. and it was about 12.20 when Det-sergeant John William Marsh, upstairs in C.I.D. section on the first floor, was told about the unusual prisoner. He came downstairs at once. By now the prisoner had been identified. He was Edward Louis John Paisnel of Maison du Soleil, Grouville, one of the eastern parishes. He was a small, but highly respected, building contractor by trade and son of a farming couple. The Paisnels were one of the oldest of Jersey families and there were vague claims to descent from one of the great feudal families who had owned tracts of land in both Normandy and Jersey in the Middle Ages; claims, certainly, which no College of Heralds would ever attempt to substantiate for it was a common thing for peasants or labourers to take the surname of their lord as it became necessary, through population growth, to adopt surnames.

Marsh's first job was to search the coat a little more thoroughly. As he was doing so, my husband was asked what he had been up to and where was he going?

'I was going to an orgy,' he replied. 'I was not involving anybody.'

Inside the rubber lining of the coat, Detective Marsh found a face mask and a roll of surgical adhesive tape. Marsh was very excited now, for all sorts of slots were being filled in in the mental picture the police had formed of the sex-fiend who had been terrorizing the island. He noticed that on each of my husband's cheeks were the remains of adhesive which indicated that the mask must have been worn that night.

'What was this for?' asked Marsh.

Ted replied: 'I was painting.'

As Detective Marsh tried to interrogate him further, my husband stopped him by saying: 'It's my coat. I'm wearing it and that's that – I'm not saying anything else about it.'

'Does your wife know about these clothes?' insisted Marsh.

'No' said Ted.

'What about the car?'

'I borrowed that,' said Ted. The police got busy checking car registrations on the island and discovered that the 1100 belonged to a Mr Charles Alfred St George, of Le Mans, Daisy Hill, Gorey who was later to tell them that he had parked the car in a field near his garage, leaving the keys in it as was his custom; no one had permission to use it.

At 12.25 a.m., Detective Inspector George Shutler came into the interview room to take charge of further inquiries. A police photographer, Detective-Sergeant D. A. McLinton was called in and photographed what Detective Marsh had already called 'this weird outfit'. Shutler set about getting all the ends tied up in what he instinctively knew was going to be the biggest case he had ever handled; what he already knew was the end of the long and amazing search for the will-o'-the-wisp who for at least eleven long years had been, not to put too fine a point on it, making a monkey out of the police.

'So I've met you at last!' were almost the first words Inspector Shutler addressed to my husband.

Detective Marsh was immediately despatched to look over the Morris 1100 where it still lay in the tomato field. A search of the

15

Morris revealed nothing incriminating or unusual – nothing unusual, that is, except a raffia cross of the type used to hand out to the congregation at Mass in a Catholic Church on Palm Sunday. Marsh was later to discover that the cross had, in fact, been made by Mr St George's daughter for a school nativity play. He could see no particular relevance in it to my husband's case and having first examined it, he then put it back where he found it. He then returned to Police Headquarters.

While he was away, my husband had been further interrogated by Detective Constable B. C. R. Simpson and by John Riseborough who took a statement. Asked about the car, Ted said: 'I found it; I won't say anything more'. Asked to account for the strange collection found on his person, he said: 'You have found them in my possession. I cannot say any more'. Detective Simpson pressed him particularly about the wig and the mask.

'They were a disguise.'

Still boxing carefully with words, my husband tried to throw the police off the scent by saying that 'orgies took place' and that he was on his way to 'a sex orgy'. Then he added, 'Several hundred years ago, they'd have burned me for this.'

'What about the wristband?' persisted Simpson.

'They're a defence.'

'Against what?' asked Simpson.

'Against judo or karate.'

It was 2.55 a.m. approximately, according to police records, when my own world fell apart and I got the first inkling that I had been married for years to a man whom normal people would rightly regard as a monster. I should add right away that though I was married to Ted Paisnel, we had ceased to live normally as man and wife as early as 1960, shortly after the birth of my daughter. Indeed, although Ted Paisnel continued to support me and my children and much of our life continued along normal lines, he had built himself separate quarters at the other end of our house and we had not occupied the same bedroom for more than a decade.

I was asleep as usual when, at almost three o'clock in the morning, I was roused by the police. Apparently, they had had some difficulty, owing to the unusual lay-out of Maison de Soleil, in finding the right door and had, indeed, climbed up a ladder at the side of the house under the impression that this gave the only access to the living quarters. The first thing I knew, therefore, was when I was aroused by this tremendous hammering on the door of my bedroom. My daughter Claudette, who slept in the same room, began screaming. I jumped out of my bed and still in my nightdress opened the bedroom door to find the corridor outside filled with policemen. They asked me to step outside and I did so.

'Where's your husband?' one of them asked.

I was in such a daze that I gave the first – and indeed, most natural answer – that came into my head. 'He's where he always is – in his office. He doesn't sleep here. He has his own place twenty yards down the lane.'

'No' they told me, 'he isn't there.'

'Well, I don't know' I said, 'what time is it? – he might be out fishing or playing cards or anything. I never worry where he is.'

Once again, they asked me where he was.

'Look' I said, 'I *don't know*! If he's not in his bed, go and find out where he is yourselves. This is where I sleep.'

They then asked me to go downstairs with them and I did so after putting on my dressing gown. In the sitting room, they told me they had arrested Ted.

'What on earth for?' I demanded.

'He stole a car and he was driving at 70 m.p.h.' said Inspector Shutler.

I said at once, 'Well, that I don't believe!' I was really pretty cross by now, for I knew Ted Paisnel's driving ability. 'I simply can't believe *that*! He can hardly drive at 15 m.p.h. never mind 70. He drives everybody mad the slow way he drives (Ted, in all the years I've known him, has been an infuriating driver – slow and insistent on hugging the crown of the road). As for driving a stolen car – he wouldn't even know how to turn the ignition on.'

Inspector Shutler gave me a wry look and said 'I'm afraid you you don't know your husband very well.'

My son by my first marriage, then came into the room and I told him that Ted had been arrested. He went white and then the police asked how old he was. When I told them he was fifteen, Inspector Shutler said: 'In that case, he's old enough to witness a search of the house.'

I ought, perhaps, to explain that Maison du Soleil is, in fact, four different establishments under what appears to be a single roof. Think of it as L-shaped. The main house, belonging to Ted's parents (his mother died within four months of her son's conviction and sentence) occupies the left hand side of the vertical part of the L and faces the main road. Ted's sister lives with her husband in a separate establishment at the rear of the main house.

17

Ted built a house for himself at right angles to the main house – in other words, the horizontal part of the L. In due course, Ted further subdivided this part. In the angle of the L, he built himself an office-bedsitter and other rooms, where he lived, while I and the children occupied the main rooms at the end of the horizontal part of the L. The part where I live gives access to the garden, but has to be approached along a lane about twenty-five yards long leading in from the main road.

It is clear, I think, that the police hoped, by breaking in on me at this hour of the morning, not only to find objects that might further incriminate my husband but also to test the extent of *my* knowledge of his activities. If I had been a party to his crimes, even if only by maintaining a silence in the face of repeated appeals by the police over the years, then they might hope to shock me into an admission of my knowledge by taking me completely unawares. As I was totally innocent – and, indeed, stunned to the very roots of my being as police investigations gradually revealed the enormity of my husband's offences – I reacted, I believe, in the only way possible. I told the police that my husband and I were married in little more than name; that none of his possessions, beyond the odd book or two, or objects held in common, such as the TV set, remained in the part of the house where I lived. Taking my son with them, Detective Inspector Shutler, Detective Sergeant Marsh and the two police constables who had originally captured my husband, went and searched Ted's quarters.

This first search revealed nothing very sensational, although the police did carry away certain objects that were to play a great part in helping them to secure a conviction against my husband. They found various clothing and a collection of headgear which included pom-pom hats such as those worn by French sailors and cloth caps of the type worn by labourers. They took away a large number of shoes and a tape-recorder with some tapes to fit it and some desk diaries and other papers. Also a bottle of after-shave lotion.

The desk diaries were quite revealing, although in no way conclusive. Under each day's date, Ted had invariably written in a job he had to do, or had done, that particular day. What was curious was that there was not a single entry on any of the days when a sex assault had taken place on the island.

One of the tapes – as the police later discovered – gave an extraordinary insight into my husband's mentality. I had known for years that he was tinkering with the idea of writing short stories, but I had not paid very much attention to this ambition. But on one of the tapes Ted had recorded a short story – a tale of unbelievable malevolence and horror and violence. It was about a child being pecked to death by a chicken. It told of a mother running down and finding this mangled body in a chicken coop. I simply could not bear to listen to it and it would be my opinion that few normally-balanced people could listen to it without feeling extremely disturbed. I remembered then that Ted had once told me that he had one of his stories accepted by the magazine *Argosy* and that when I had asked him the subject, he had replied, 'Oh, a horror story – they fascinate me.' I had not paid all that much attention to the remark, nor indeed, to his claim that *Argosy* had printed it – a yarn, I ought to add, which had no foundation.

The after-shave lotion was a cheap, readily-available brand and, to me, would not have appeared to carry much significance. However, Detective Marsh later poured some of this lotion on a piece of cottonwool and asked one of Ted's boy victims to smell it. The boy was able at once to identify the scent as similar to that given off by his assailant, thus forging another, if in itself a fragile, link in the chain of circumstantial evidence that was eventually to convict my husband.

The police also took away some rubber padding similar to that inside the coat my husband had been wearing – Detective Marsh felt it might be useful in case Ted attempted to deny ownership of the coat in court. They were about to leave when Marsh noticed a piece of cottonwool lying on the floor. I must say I would never have dreamed that such a common object could have any particular significance but Detective Marsh remembered something. He had apparently interviewed a boy who had been attacked by a sex-fiend in 1963 and the boy had described his assailant as wearing 'white bushy eyebrows'. What struck Marsh about the bit of cottonwool was that it was arched in such a way as to look like a frosted eyebrow of the Father Christmas type. When he found this, he had really little further doubt that the years of searching and frustration, so far as the police were concerned, were over; that they had at last nailed their man.

Not that even the apprehension of my husband was to make the life of the Jersey States police any easier. When Inspector Shutler and his team left my house that morning, they found themselves plunged abruptly into a murder hunt. The body of a young red-headed girl had been found by a courting couple on one of the Jersey beaches at 2 a.m. She lay on her back with her hot pants suit torn and she had been strangled.

Only one thing was certain; whether my husband Ted Paisnel was or was not the sex-fiend who had carried out some twenty-one voilent sex assaults in Jersey over the previous decade, he was not responsible for this one.

TWO

THE SECRET ROOM

I cannot remember sleeping at all that dreadful night when I learned that my husband had been picked up by the police who, though holding him only on technical charges concerned with driving offences, seemed to be convinced that they were on to something much more sinister. For over an hour they continued their searches and interrogation. It was almost 4.30 a.m., Detective Marsh says, before the police party returned to H.Q. only to find themselves involved in yet another murder hunt (for they still had the unsolved murder of a Finnish au pair girl in 1966 on their books).

I was so numbed by events that I could only follow my usual routine. I had arranged for my daughter to have a riding lesson over in the parish of St Peter that morning and I went through with it as planned although my thoughts were in a turmoil. On the way back, I had an impulse to talk to Ted so that although I knew I had a right to see him only during normal prison visiting hours, I made a detour and called at the gaol. It took a little persuasion before I was admitted and ushered into the presence of my husband. I don't quite know what I had expected to see, other than a man nervous, distraught, possibly broken by a night-long interrogation and under a terrible strain at the thought of the charges that might be impending.

To my astonishment, Ted was his usual cheerful self. I might have been visiting a man who had been admitted to hospital for some minor operation rather than a man who had been caught in the most suspicious of circumstances. I could scarcely believe my eyes.

'What on earth is all this about?' I began. 'Do you realize what we've all been through during the night – hours of questioning and the whole house upset. What on earth have you been doing?'

'Oh, don't worry, luv,' said Ted. 'It's just one of those things. I got into a car at the end of a field and I thought it was mine and I drove around. Oh, don't worry about it – I drove too fast.'

21

He could obviously see that I was still very upset and dissatisfied. 'Don't worry, I tell you – they've got the wrong man, that's all' he assured me after I had told him how Inspector Shutler had described the strange garb he was alleged to have been wearing. What could I do in the circumstances ? There was my husband, the same cheery, kind-hearted Ted I had always known, reassuring me in his usual easy fashion. A man less likely to be guilty of anything serious, I had never seen. Such, of course, is the power of familiarity; the refusal of a mind used to normality to accept the abnormal when it wears the same face as everyone else. I simply went home and cried.

That afternoon, the police called again. They talked to me and I understand they also interviewed Ted's parents. They also had another look-round Ted's workshop which Detective Marsh described in court as 'giving the appearance of being used as a bedsitter. There was bed linen on a couch and crockery and food on a dresser'.

One of the most remarkable things about this remarkable case was the way that Detective Marsh's intuition refused to give him any rest. At 7.30 that evening, accompanied by Detective Colin Lang, he was back at Maison du Soleil under the nagging compulsion 'that we had missed something' – 'one of those police intuitions, I suppose ?' suggested the Attorney General at the trial.

The two men, I have since found, turned over the room again, but could find nothing that would in anyway definitely link my husband with the sex crimes that had both horrified and terrorized the island for at least twelve years; years during which it was not considered safe for a woman or child to be out after dark and when many family men slept with revolvers under their pillows despite having bolted and shuttered all doors and windows – the Monster, they had learned to their cost, seemed to be able to come and go like a ghost.

With almost a sense of sheer desperation, they began to lift down and leaf through Ted's library of books. Not the least remarkable qualities about Ted Paisnel is his obsession with literature. He is a simply tremendous reader and most of his reading matter is anything but trash. Marsh and Lang found themselves ploughing through what they themselves call 'heavy' material. There were books on English literature; on European history; books on judo, karate, palmistry, hypnotism; a variety of books on political subjects, including studies of Communism and books on various aspects of medicine and other texts. There were also very much less considerable works – sensational fiction by a writer called Dennis Wheatley who has specialized to some extent in writing thrillers with a background of Black magic; fiction with the titles 'The Devil – this' or 'The Devil – that'. There were also a number of fairly seriously-written books. These included books on devilry and torture including Eric Maple's *The Dark World of Witches* and Emlyn Williams book on the Moors Murders. There was also *The Satanic Mass* and an extremely rare book called *The Black Baron* worth several hundred pounds sterling, on the life and crimes of Gilles de Rais. None of this seemed to the detectives of anything more than passing interest and they might easily have decided to leave the books where they were had it not been for an interesting discovery which Detective Marsh then made.

By an almost inexplicable oversight, no one, during the two previous searches had thought to pull back a red curtain which hung down against the wall in one of the corners of the room. At first sight, indeed, the curtain seemed to have little more than an ornamental use, like a tapestry. Almost idly, Detective Marsh pulled it back.

What he saw then, staggered him. Whatever he had expected to find behind that curtain certainly exceeded anything he would usually have allowed his practical, down-to-earth, imagination to encompass. The parted curtain revealed an alcove a foot or two deep. The wall of the alcove was padded from top to bottom with dark carpet-underfelt. Affixed to this were a number of simple and unremarkable if, in the context of their positioning, rather inexplicable objects. The first and most remarkable object, right at the top and pointing downwards, was a large wooden dagger or knife. Under this, also hanging, was a round glass bowl. Under this again, was a little shelf on which rested a glass jar full of cloves, a glass chalice and a china toad.

'Come here and have a look at this' said Marsh to Lang, 'What do you make of this – it seems to me like an altar or shrine of some sort ?'

Whether or not his brief perusal of 'literature' on the Black Arts had anything to do with this leaping deduction Marsh is unable to say. An alert man, a cockney by birth, who speaks very fast and thinks even faster, Detective Marsh was not the kind of man to reject the unusual simply because it was not run-of-the-mill. Everything about this case, too, had borne, to say the least of it, all the hallmarks of something unusually weird. It was, in fact, a logical enough jump to associate this shrine – for what else could it mean ? – with some form of witchcraft. That, of course, would have to be checked; authorities on the occult would have to be consulted.

Marsh, in fact, found his mind racing with thoughts of a most improbable nature. The dagger, for example; the wooden dagger. He remembered that during an attack on a boy back in 1963, the victim had been forced by his assailant to kiss a wooden object hanging from the man's belt. At the time, the Jersey detective had concluded that the assailant was possibly a religious nut of some sort who had forced the boy to kiss a crucifix. Indeed, in pursuit of this line of inquiry, Marsh had been among the team who had descended on the local Catholic priest and 'bounced him' on the matter; very much, indeed, to the poor priest's surprise.

'Remember the boy who was made to kiss a wooden object ?' asked Marsh and Lang nodded. 'It wasn't a crucifix at all! I'll bet it was that dagger.' The dagger, too, would provide an explanation of the strange sheath that Ted had been wearing on his belt the night of his capture. Even as he thought this, Detective Marsh's mind was racing on to an even weirder idea. He remembered the raffia cross he had found in the Morris 1100. If Ted were a witch who had summoned the powers of Evil to aid him in his nefarious designs and to escape arrest all these years, had he been trapped by the cross ? To anyone who believed in the power of Good to overcome Evil, it seemed much more than a coincidence that on the night he stole a car with, unknown to him, a cross in it, he should have made his first – and only – mistake. What, if it had not been the forces ranged against Evil, had caused Ted to 'jump' the traffic lights at the very moment when a police car was there ? Why, when he knew he was being pursued by the police, and he not stopped and slipped out of his incriminating nail-spiked coat before apologizing to the police ? Why, unless again, the powers of Light had finally decided to fight off his Evil, had Ted, out of the 45,000 registered vehicles on Jersey that summer evening, stolen the only vehicle carrying a cross ?

Detective Marsh quickly put such ideas out of his mind and got down to the much more prosaic, if less fascinating, task of finding evidence of a more substantial nature which could be brought against my husband in open court. Ted Paisnel might

24

or might not practice witchcraft, white or black. But to prove him a witch was one thing; to prove that he was the man who was the Monster of Jersey was another. Encouraged by the discovery of the shrine, both men redoubled their efforts and began banging on the wall of the alcove, which gave off a hollow sound. While one pulled and tugged at the wall, the other continued to bang and within a few seconds, they were rewarded. The back of the alcove gave about a quarter of an inch at the bottom. Pulling at both top and bottom, they managed to open what were, in effect the doors of a cupboard. Then they noticed that behind the top shelf of this cupboard, there was a hole. They struck a match to have a better look but as soon as they placed it near the whole, the draught blew it out and they realized that this was some kind of a keyhole, probably. with a considerable space behind, A search of my husband's room, however, failed to reveal any key that might have opened this door (there was, in fact, one in the room, but it had fallen down from its place and was lodged out of sight behind a shelf in another part of the room). Both detectives kept tugging away at the back of the cupboard, not really knowing what they were searching for when suddenly there was an extraordinary interruption.

A Miss Florence Hawkins, an ex-nurse, who has publicly admitted that she was my husband's mistress, arrived at Boulivot and entered Ted's workshop while the police were still trying to penetrate the secret door. Detective Marsh, with some degree of understatement, later described her behaviour to the Royal Court as 'very agitated' when she found out what they were trying to do. 'She got right upset' is how he usually puts it and it was her suspicious behaviour that made him and Detective Lang redouble their efforts to see what was on the other side. Then she declared: 'I know there was something behind that, but there's nothing there now; it was all sealed up. There used to be a room behind it. I've been in – it's empty.' She volunteered to help open it and the two detectives stepped back and allowed her to take a crack. She kept fumbling about for a few minutes until the two men lost patience and asked her desist. As Detective Marsh puts it: 'She then made a right nuisance of herself and Colin finally had to chuck her out.'

It took the two policemen one hour and twenty minutes to open up the back of the cupboard. Marsh was standing on a chair tugging away at the top and Lang was working at the bottom and both were tugging and pulling furiously when suddenly the wood split. By the light streaming in from the room where they were working, they could see a wardrobe affair and hanging up, in plain view, a long fawn raincoat, lined in red.

Marsh and Lang were now almost besides themselves, for over the years the Monster's victims had invariably described him as wearing 'a fawn coat or macintosh.'

'We were actually a bit frightened to go in there,' says Marsh today, 'because it was dark and we couldn't see.' But the whole of the cupboard swung back on two hinges and, as Marsh puts it: 'The smell! Somebody a number of years had said that their assailant had given off a strong, musty kind of smell – and when you smell it, you'll know it. I've been back a few times and the smell is still there.' I myself can substantiate Detective Marsh's statement; the smell is still there and seems at times almost overpowering. I recollect now that there was always a musty smell about Ted's clothes.

Despite their reluctance to enter, both detectives went into my husband's secret room and had a close-up look at the extremely incriminating fawn raincoat. On the floor lay the belt. Hanging up was a dark blue track suit and on a shelf there was a cloth cap with the lining missing together with a brown home-made wig, with a bit of Jersey Evening Post of 14th March, 1969 stuck inside it. There were also a pair of rubber ankle boots, a camera and another cap. Examining the 'secret door', the two men discovered that it had been fitted with a strong barrel-type mortice bolt at the top and it was not, indeed, until several weeks later that Detective Marsh found the key of the lock on a ledge behind a cabinet in the outer room.

Neither detective wanted to touch anything until Inspector Shutler had seen the secret room and a police photographer had taken the necessary pictures. So Marsh stayed on while Detective Lang went back to H.Q. to report on what they had found. Marsh says that as he waited there in the growing darkness, an overpowering sense of something eerie or evil seemed to grip him. He admits that it might well have been imagination on his part, but despite his considerable physical build and his courage in tackling all kinds of normal police hazards, he could not help feeling nervously uncomfortable. The sense of something abnormal, weird, even supernatural was heightened by the curious blue light that seemed to flood my husband's secret room. Every object, even the wooden dagger, seemed to have a bluish tinge, possibly because so much of the room was painted blue. Later, Detective Marsh was astonished to discover that almost everything my husband owned had been painted blue – saws, hammers, all the tools of his contracting trade, garden implements, the lot, were in one way or another, daubed with blue paint. Ted later told him that he had painted everything blue because that was the colour of the sky and therefore represented 'freedom'. But at that moment, there in that strange room, the thought that it might represent 'freedom' did not occur to Detective Marsh. He found himself almost involuntarily leaving the room and going outside the building to wait for Inspector Shutler and the other police to arrive.

I was brought down and shown the shrine or altar, after the police had warned me, 'Brace yourself, we're going to show you something.' My reaction was the obvious one of amazement, particularly when I saw this curved wooden dagger or knife. Then Inspector Shutler said, 'This is an official question – have you ever been in this room before?' They swung back the cupboard door and showed me the secret room. One of the detectives, after I had shaken my head, stepped into the room and grabbing the black spiky wig, handed it to me. 'Is this yours?' asked Mr Shutler and again I shook my head, too numb, really, to think clearly. I was told afterwards that Florence Hawkins, who I did not notice was in the room, smiled at my horror.

I stood there while the police continued their search. They almost tore the ottoman on which Ted slept apart. In the cupboard compartment of this they found a collection of newspaper clippings. They were all from the more sensational London Sunday newspapers and referred to the murders of beautiful young girls – I remember that one headline said, 'She was a beauty – now she's dead?' I repeated that I knew nothing of all this, that I had never even been in this part of the house before. My son, however, said he knew about the secret room. 'That's where Dad used to keep his paints' he told Mr Shutler. 'I saw it when it was being built.' A little while later that night, when my daughter inquired what the fuss was about and I told her about the secret room, she said, 'Oh, yes, I saw that a long time ago – Daddy used to keep tins of paint in it'. The police also discovered an old organ down there, which Ted later said he had bought in a sale, and Claudette said that when she used to take Ted's letters down to him (they always arrived in my part of the house) that she played on it. Until that moment, however, I had no idea it existed.

While the official police photographer was taking photographs of Ted's office, the black magic shrine and the secret room with its contents, Detectives Shutler, Marsh and Lang climbed a ladder which led to a loft over the secret room. Among the valuable items of evidence discovered were approximately 100 photographs which they took away to examine in detail. One, in particular, was to prove extremely incriminating to Ted. This was of a house in the Rue de Chateau Clairvale, in the parish of St Saviour's, where a nine-year-old boy had been assaulted on 19th April 1963. Later inquiries showed that the picture must have been taken between 1957 and 1960, because until 1957 the house had been painted a different colour and *after* 1960, it had a TV aerial. The angle of the camera shot was very unusual, too; hardly the angle a resident would have chosen if he had wanted to show how nice his house was or a house-agent to show what a desirable property he had to sell; it was taken from behind a bush and even to the uninitiated eye bore all the marks of having been taken surreptitiously.

What staggered the police, though, was the extraordinary gap of time between the taking of the photograph and the assault on the boy. Ted had actually planned the assault *years* before he carried it out. Such a degree of premeditation was so highly unusual that it was no wonder the police had found him such a will-o'-the-wisp. At the time, they had proceeded on the usual police assumption that the miscreant would have felt impelled to carry out his attack within *days* of marking down the house. They had, in fact, extended their inquiries, which took the form of asking about suspicious strangers or workmen seen in the vicinity, well beyond a matter of days; well beyond weeks, indeed. Questioning the boy's parents and residents in the vicinity, they had gone back more than *six months*, but the inquiries, naturally, had drawn a blank. For a man so cold-bloodedly to plot a crime of this nature several years ahead of its committal broke every rule in the book of police experience. Such was my husband's cunning.

That night, however, armed with the result of their searches, the police went back to their headquarters leaving me and my distraught little family in a state bordering on extreme distress. On the other hand, as Detective Marsh has described it, the police felt 'very happy' with themselves. All the bits and pieces were falling neatly into place, although there was still a long hard slog ahead of them before they could charge Ted Paisnel with anything more than a series of motoring offences.

However, it is a well-known fact of police life that once you have 'put a name on the books', in other words, arrested someone, an investigation usually takes on a radically different aspect. Everything that has been previously obscure and inchoate becomes clear and comprehensible. In more down to earth terms, witnesses begin to come forward to volunteer information that invariably helps the C.I.D. to sew up their loose ends. People who had been nursing their own little bits of the jig-saw come forward with their contributions to help complete the total picture.

Not the least remarkable aspect of the case, from the police point of view anyway, was that absolutely no one came forward to volunteer anything. Detectives Marsh and Lang, for example, not only found that people would not volunteer information, but, indeed, refused to give it when pressed. 'We went to see people who had been attacked in the past and they actually chucked us out of their houses' says Detective Marsh. 'They simply didn't want to know. One bloke was going to punch us on the nose; another ordered us out of the house; another said he had a number of kids now and didn't want to know. One man, whose wife had done nothing but shout when her boy had been attacked, wouldn't give us the time of day. Throughout Jersey, you almost got the impression that there were a whole lot of people who simply didn't want to see Ted Paisnel charged.'

It was a silence, even at that early stage of the investigation, which to the police seemed more than a little ominous. Marsh and Lang, at least, pondered on the widespread fear of black magic in the superstitious life of many Jersey people.

I went to see Ted in prison again the next day and once again I left feeling absolutely certain that the police were barking up the wrong tree. He was his usual cheery self, exuding complete innocence and, apparently, supremely confident that he would get away with it.

'Don't worry, luv,' he reassured me again, 'I'll be out of here in a little while and if they accuse me of anything, I'll sue them to the hilt – so don't worry a bit.'

That, may I add, was a lot easier said than done.

'But what about this black magic thing then?' I asked, and described the shrine which the police had uncovered.

Ted brushed this off after his usual casual and persuasive fashion, 'Oh, don't worry about that, luv – that's got nothing to do with you. I've always been interested in that. But just because I belong to a club, that doesn't make me a criminal, does it ?'

I agreed it didn't but asked him what kind of club.

'Oh, it's a secret society.'

'Yes, but what kind ?'

'Well, we're not allowed to know each other's identities – that's why we wear masks.' He then added that he loved me and to take care of your children and 'not to forget your flu injection.'

I left the prison that day so absolutely certain that Ted was innocent that when I got back home, I rang Inspector Shutler and in a state of absolute distress insisted that they allow Ted to go. I remember sobbing down the telephone, 'How dare you put us all through this when he simply belongs to a club. You must know you haven't got the right man!'

I was in such a distressed state, indeed, that the three detectives arrived at my house within ten minutes of the telephone call and proceeded to do their best not only to calm me down, but to convince me, beyond any reasonable doubt, that he was the guilty man. They showed me some rather horrible pictures of the children Ted was alleged to have assaulted, with great marks or weals across their backs which the police, backed up later by medical evidence, believed could have been made only by the wrist bands Ted had been wearing on the night of his arrest. 'There is no doubt that he's the Monster of Jersey' said Inspector Shutler, 'We're absolutely convinced we've got the right man and whatever your feelings, you must accept this'. He then showed me a picture of Ted taken shortly after his arrest. I was astonished; the man in the photograph was not the Ted I knew; this man had a *cruel* look. Inspector Shutler asked me gently, 'Is that your husband ?'

I could only stumble out the words, 'Well, it doesn't look like him.'

'Well' said Mr Shutler, 'that's what he really looks like.'

It was at this meeting, so far as I can remember, that Inspector Shutler suddenly held up a photostat copy of a letter the police had received in August 1966, a few days before a 15-year-old girl had been criminally assaulted and raped at Trinity Manor. The year 1966 had been a particularly bad year for sex crimes, for in December of that year – indeed, on New Year's Eve – the body of a Finnish *au pair* girl called Tuula Hoeoek, aged 20, who had been living in the house of Major-General and Mrs L. C. Thomas, of Forrest Hill, Beaumont, had been found battered to death, after having been raped, in a field in the parish of St Clement.

This letter was the second, in the same handwriting, that the police had received from the sex-fiend over the years. The first one, received in 1960, had simply said, 'I see you're offering a reward for me, the man in the duffle coat' (I shall detail the significance of this later). The 1966 letter was couched in very different terms. Ted had become so confident that he felt impelled to tease the police and wrote to them as follows:

My Dear Sir,
   I think that it is just the time to tell you that you are just wasting your time, you will never be able to catch me as every time I have done wat I always intended to do and remember it will not stop at this, but I will be fair to you and give you a chance. I have never had much out of this life but I intend to get everything I can now. . . .
   I have always wanted to do the perfect crime. I have done this, but this time let the moon shine very britte in September because this time it must be perfect, not one but two. I am not a maniac by a long shot but I like to play with you people. You will hear from me before September and I will give you all the clues. Just to see if you can catch me.
                              Yours very sincerely
                                   Wait and See.

Inspector Shutler held the photostat a few feet – far enough to prevent the actual words being read – from the face of my eldest daughter – my first child by my previous marriage. She was very fond of Ted, as fond of him as if he had been her natural father, and she was very well acquainted with his hand-writing. Practising handwriting, indeed, had always been one of Ted's favourite past-times; he was continually shaping and practising new capital letters and that sort of thing.

Quite involuntarily, and without being able to make out the actual sense of the letter, my daughter exclaimed, after Mr Shutler asked her if she had ever seen it before, 'Ah, what's Ted been writing now?' She was able not only to recognize the handwriting but even the curious phraseology he had used. Instead of writing, as most people would, 'Dear Sir', he had followed his invariable practice and begun the letter 'My Dear Sir'.

On Thursday, 15th July 1971, at 3 p.m., acting on the instructions of the Attorney-General of Jersey, Det-Inspector George Shutler and Detectives Marsh and Lang interviewed my husband in prison. Ted's defence counsel, Advocate Dorey, was also present. Inspector Shutler began by enumerating the various objects which had been found at Maison du Soleil. Ted did not seem in the slightest put out.

'That's right. Why shouldn't they be there? They weren't covered.'

'What about the track suit?' This had an important bearing on a recent assault.

'Oh, I've never worn that,' said Ted off-handedly. 'I've kept it – but I don't wear it.'

Mr Shutler then asked him about the secret room.

'It wasn't a secret room' protested Ted vehemently, 'It was put up by a carpenter (whom he named) who fitted up the cupboard door. He is now in England and another man (whom he also named) helped him. My son knew about the room, and so did my father probably.'

Asked to explain the wig, Ted said he had discussed this already. 'There was a bit of paper inside. The track suit and other articles are mine. That is all I am going to say. People have been interfering with us and have been "mugging" us up. My little friends have been interfered with by people who interfered with me.' He then volunteered the information that he had put nails in his coat so that 'people could not attack us. It was a defence.'

Asked to explain why the lining was missing from the cap, he demanded to know, 'what was wrong with the cap?' To the question, had he ever worn the cap with a wig, he gave the explanation, 'No. They did not go together, do they?' (the police thought they did). He added that he 'kept a lot of old shoes and clothes'.

Questioned about the fawn raincoat, he said, 'I got it at a sale, probably at Langlois, when I bought a trunk of old clothing.' (A police check revealed no such purchase, at least under his own name.)

'What about the cord found in your pocket?' asked Detective Marsh. At first, the police had not attached any great significance to the pyjama cord. Although the Monster had made several attempts to strangle some of his victims, it hardly seemed likely that ordinary pyjama cord would have had the necessary strength; it was too likely to snap. On the other hand, it was certainly true that many victims had identified their assailant as wearing 'a fawn raincoat, tied round the waist with string'. Could the string have been pyjama cord? Even more fascinating, when they finally perused *The Satanic Mass*, one of the books found in Ted's office during the critical third search, Marsh and Lang discovered that the symbol of the cord had great significance in black witchcraft; it signified the umbilical cord – life or death.

Ted's easy answer was that it was 'only a bit of pyjama cord which was shoved in my pocket when I was working at someone's farm'. As for the lengths of sashcord, he 'used these to start the lawn mower or my concrete mixer'. His answers were nothing, if not ingenious.

Mr Marsh queried him again about the nails in his coat.

'Oh, I only put those in a few weeks ago.' They were a protection when he was climbing up and down the roofs of buildings, making sure that the rope up which he hoisted himself did not slip.

'It's your coat, all right, isn't it?'

Ted resolutely refused to commit himself.

'What about the mask, then?'

'That was given to me – it belongs to a meeting I go to.' He refused to say exactly who had given it to him. As for the incriminating wig, that had also been 'given to me', but again he refused to say by whom.

The wristbands, with the nails protruding? 'That was an idea I'd had. But I don't know why I had them on that night – I was drugged up at the time, Dr Georgelin will say why. The amount of drugs I took must have had an effect on me for what I did that evening.' What, exactly, were the drugs for? 'They're for losing weight, tranquillizers and for muscular treatment' – this was the result of an injury, he claimed, when he had been working as a coal miner in Wales. Ted often walked with a limp.

He then reverted to the wristbands again. He used them, he said, 'for scratching a wall' during the course of plastering operations. He had never worn them outside his own house before that night; but he had worn them inside his own home when 'talking to a chappie about judo'.

The States of Jersey analyst had been busy with Ted's possessions in the five days since his arrest and the police now had a few less than gentle shocks to administer. Important breakthroughs had been made medically in 1963 with regard to secretors in blood groupings; thus it had become possible to identify a man's blood group via any semen stains he might leave. Ted was told that both his raincoat and his track suit had been analysed; that seminal stains had been found on both. Worse, from his point of view, the stains were unquestionably proof that whoever had left them – and it was hardly likely that it was not he – had the same blood group, O. Fibres and a pubic hair, which matched his own, had also been taken from the bed of one of his victims. Blood had also been found on the nails of the wristbands.

'Go on!' said Ted to Detective Marsh. 'How is that explained? You are trying to say it is human blood. It is animal blood.' He added that his dog had been on the raincoat and the track suit while they were in the car, implying that the seminal stains were caused by the dog. The blood on them? – for there were slight blood marks. 'The dog has had bones on it' and Ted, implying that the blood marks were from the bones.

Inspector Shutler then explained that police inquiries were now centred on an attack on a boy in the Vallée des Vaux area, in the parish of St Helier, which had taken place on the night of 9th August 1970.

'The description fits you to a T – right down to the mask, the after-shave lotion, dark clothing which could be the track suit and the fawn raincoat with string' Inspector Shutler told him. 'Everything fits in perfectly.' The police, in fact, were not too sure about the mask. All the boy had been able to tell them was that his assailant had worn either a faded khaki handkerchief tied round his face or a mask – he had not been able to make out which clearly in the dark. All he knew, indeed, was that the man had kept lifting up the side of the mask or the faded khaki scarf or handkerchief in order to speak. When Inspector Shutler explained that the boy had identified a mask or a faded khaki scarf of the same colour, Ted was quick to seize his opportunity.

'That's different from a mask, isn't it?'

Where, by the way, had he been that night?

'I was sleeping with Miss Hawkins that night. I usually go there about six o'clock in the evening. I believe I was issued with a parking ticket that night.' He's got a good memory, thought Detective Marsh – perhaps too good (and, in fact, a police check failed to reveal that any parking ticket had been issued against him on that occasion).

'What about last Saturday night?' asked Inspector Shutler abruptly. This was the night of his arrest.

'Ah, last Saturday night was different, wasn't it?' said Ted wryly.

Under interrogation, my husband, in fact, began to grow noticeably less cocky and before the interview was ended, he was to exhibit signs of some distress. The police pursued the interrogation relentlessly.

'Do you deny being the man who attacked the boy in Vallée des Vaux?'

'I deny being the man who did it' said Ted, 'and you'll have a hell of a job to prove it!'

'What about the seminal stains on the raincoat?'

'I've had intercourse in the car.'

'You haven't slept with your wife for ten years, we understand – so she says.'

'That's right – but the dog's been on the raincoat and has had his bones on it as well.'

'What if the blood marks we found on it *are human*?'

'I doubt if they are' insisted Ted.

My husband then started, as Detective Marsh put it, 'to talk about the secret society and his "friends"'.

'Tell us' one of the detectives asked, 'If it's a secret society and you all wear masks so that nobody knows anybody else in the society, how do you meet in the first place to become a member?'

'I won't involve anybody else' said Ted firmly, 'they all come of their own free will.'

'How long have you been a member of this secret society?' inquired Mr Marsh.

'A long time.'

'How long?'

'Before 1949.'

Ted then went on to add vehemently, 'I don't care if I get one, five or ten years in prison, I'll still be alive and eating and breathing and you can't shoot me. If you can prove any of these offences and it goes to court, well, then, that's it, I can't involve anybody else.'

With a nod to Advocate Dorey, Mr Shutler then told Ted that he was going to charge him with the assault on the boy who lived in Vallée des Vaux. Ted took the news philosophically.

'That's understandable – but all you've got against me are the stains on the coat.'

Inspector Shutler then began questioning him about a whole series of sexual crimes against young children and Ted's confidence began to evaporate perceptibly. Before the end of the interview, indeed he was to become, as Detective Marsh describes it, 'nervous as hell.' His left leg was crossed over his right, his right leg was shaking and he had his right arm clutched under his armpit – 'you'd think he was going to take off – he just couldn't control himself.' He had not quite reached this stage yet, however, and with an attempt at bravado declared, 'Well, they are not little kids now. Go on, go on, go ahead and prove it!'

Inspector Shutler, instead, raised the question of the boastful letter received by the police in August 1966, claiming that the writer intended committing the 'perfect crime'. This, he pointed out, had arrived a few days after a young girl had been attacked in the parish of Trinity; furthermore, pointed out Mr Shutler, Ted's step-daughter had identified the handwriting as his.

'Oh, that was only a photocopy' laughed Ted nervously, and then, quite abruptly, clammed up. Satisfied that they had got as much out of him as they were likely to get at that meeting, the three policemen rose to go.

They had reached the door when a sudden thought struck Detective Marsh. At this stage, he had no clear idea how the raffia cross found in the Morris 1100 on the night of Ted's arrest, fitted into the case – if at all. On a sudden impulse, however Marsh took the raffia cross from the bag in which he was carrying various papers and showed it to Ted.

'Is this yours?' he demanded.

The three policemen were utterly astonished by the sudden change that came over Ted. 'He almost jumped over the table' is how Detective Marsh describes it. 'His eyes nearly popped out of his head, his face went a deep red and he began to chuckle in a strange manner.' Then Ted declared, 'My master would laugh very long and loud at this.'

Certain now that the black magic aspects were one of the keys to the whole case, Detective-Sergeant Colin Lang who, with Detective Marsh had spent almost every minute of what ought to have been their leisure time since the discovery of the secret room in reading through Ted's library, asked, 'How about the toad?'

'That's part of something' was all Ted would say. Then he demanded, 'Were there any cloves in there?'

'Tell us about the cloves?' prompted Detective Lang.

'No, that's my business' answered Ted, shaking his head.

'Tell us about the wooden knife, then?'

'I've told you before about that' insisted Ted.

There was then a short pause before Detective Lang, pointing to the raffia cross, asked him straight, 'Are you afraid of the cross?'

Ted shrugged. 'No, not particularly – there's a much more powerful emblem than that!'

'Touch the cross, then!' demanded Sergeant Lang. Ted, however, refused to touch it.

'You know, that's why you're here!' Detective Marsh informed him.

Ted indicated neither belief nor disbelief. All he said was, 'Your world is shrinking – our cocoon is getting larger'. Then he added a vague remark again about 'my friends' but refused to elaborate any further.

THREE

ISLAND OF DARK MYSTERIES

Bright sunshine and lovely scenery make our holiday isle one of the last places a visitor would normally associate with witchcraft or with the kind of horrible crimes for which my husband has been sentenced. This, despite a long history of witchcraft in the island and the fact that even today, if you ask farming people for an explanation of certain projecting dripstones originally installed on thatched farmhouses to prevent water seeping down the side of a chimney, you will be told they are 'witches' stones', put there to provide a passing witch with a resting place.

Jersey, a British island, lies a hundred miles south of Portland Bill in that great bay which separates Brittany and Normandy and is only fifteen miles from the coast of France. It squats in the sea like a rough, jagged platter tilted north to south to catch the rays of the sun and, by all the surface evidences, seems as innocent as Eden. To visitors it is a marvellous playground, in particular attracting honeymooners. Even to those of us who live on the island, it bears many of the characteristics of an earthly paradise. It enjoys a blaze of luxuriant growth by virtue of its latitude, excellent rainfall and the presence of the Gulf Stream. It has a Mediterranean touch about it at times. Palm trees and eucalyptus flourish and it is a riot of flowers at all seasons. Spring daffodils burgeon alongside Lenten lilies; mimosa and magnolia and the rare Jersey orchid come into bloom early and in summer, the hard granite walls enclosing the well-farmed fields are hung with the tiny daisy called the Mexican Fleabane while everywhere there are lovely banks of mesembryanthemum. Even the dankness of autumn is relieved by the famed Jersey lily. Sand dunes are bright with bushes of silver grey, laden with sweet-smelling spikes of yellow lupin flowers. Camellias blaze at Christmas.

Jersey, too, possesses what are probably some of the most glorious beaches in Europe; the Royal Bay of Grouville, St Aubin's Bay, the Bays of St Brelade, St Clement and St Ouen as well as Havre des Pas and Portelet Bay and, in the north, Grève le Lecq with its lovely reddish-coloured sand. Everywhere, if more particularly along the northern coast, there are stunning cliffs, honeycombed with more than 300 caves or with great pinnacles of rock rising out of the sea, such as the seventy-foot Needle Rock. There is a wild profusion of picturesque islets – L'Islet on which stands romantic Elizabeth Castle, linked by a breakwater to the Hermitage Rock; the Ile au Guerdain in Portelet Bay; or the islet in St Ouen's Bay on which stands La Rocca Tower, a famous landmark used by the Germans during the Occupation in the Second World War for gunnery target practice.

This island supports a resident population of about 72,000 people – many of them wealthy Englishmen who settled here to escape British taxation. Each summer, however it is almost overwhelmed by a half-million visitors, yet despite the growth of hotels, villas, shops and other built-up areas, the real Jersey essentially remains a land of farmers. Many of the farms are quite small, often not more than ten acres, with small fields each bearing its own name such as Le Grand Clos, Le Petit Clos, Le Clos de Devant and so on. But if the farms are small, the farmers themselves are relatively prosperous, mainly because every crop is ready for market in Britain long before the home-grown product can reach Covent Garden. Today, the great staple crop is probably tomatoes; in summer, rows of tomato plants with their bamboo sticks are as much a feature of rural Jersey as vineyards are to the Champagne or Bordeaux regions of France.

Yet the beauty and the tranquility of the Jersey countryside are totally deceptive which, to my mind, is a sad thing. Crime has more than doubled in the last five years and the island has become a satellite of London's underworld with more than its fair share of international racketeers. Scotland Yard's intelligence branch knows that several major bank and strong-room robberies that have taken place recently in London were planned in Jersey and that the island's banks are a refuge for 'hot' money well beyond the reach of the British tax collectors.

In a recent conspiracy trial at the Old Bailey for example, in which three defendants were convicted of importing cannabis, worth almost £800,000 on the black market, it was revealed that the smugglers had lodged all their money in a Jersey bank.

In recent years, too, there have been at least three brutal murders on the island, one of which remains unsolved although the police, I understand, are certain of the murderer's identity and hope, eventually, to be able to pin the crime on him.

Beneath the deceptively calm surface of Jersey life, therefore, lurk many dark secrets. The older Jersey families, to begin with, are closely inbred – too inbred to be entirely healthy. Ted's parents, for example, were first cousins. Relationships of an incestuous nature are common, as frequently happens in remote, isolated communities; and despite the avalanche of visitors in summer, the real Jersey folk remain largely remote and isolated. Homosexuality is also rampant. A T.V. journalist on the island who keeps a close watch on activities here, says, 'There's no doubt that Jersey has everything England has, and then a bit more in some ways. One cannot doubt, anymore than one can prove, that there are black and white magic circles at work in the island; just as there are wife-swapping parties, blue film showings and drug-taking orgies. I think the only difference between England and Jersey is that over here the witchcraft is the genuine thing, a true relic of the Old Religion rather than just an excuse for a sex orgy or a bit of wife-swapping.'

Much of the gossip on the island is certainly of a macabre nature. Everyone *knows*, I think, someone who, to put it mildly, is 'susceptible' to witchcraft. If these people do not actually practise it, their conversation is full of allusions to it; they appear to accept the premises of witchcraft. I am certain that Ted's mother, from various hints she dropped over the years, was acquainted with practising witches. His father will also tell you openly that he has seen animals struck dead as the result of a witch's curse – and many islanders relate corroborative tales. There are also many people who have seen what they take to be evidence of witchcraft – cats or cockerels found lying along roadsides with their throats cut.

White magic, of course, need not necessarily be considered macabre; in a sense, I suppose, the various faith-healers – Jersey is full of faithhealers and people who believe in faith-healers – are only practising a version of white witchcraft, but many aspects of black magic would certainly come within my definition of the macabre. Yet I am thinking of something even more bizarre, however. There is a man on the island, for example, who is said to keep the mummy of his mother in an iron chest in his home. A couple involved in a black magic circle, I've also been told, regularly choose to make love in a coffin. This is hearsay, of course; I have no way of knowing whether or not there is anything

40

more substantial to these allegations than rumour but I think they are significant of the inner life of Jersey; a life-style very different from that familiar to most holiday-makers who see Jersey as no more than a playground and its people as no more than an easy-going bunch out to make their stay as pleasant as possible.

Like England, indeed, sex crimes are not all that unusual in Jersey; nor was Ted Paisnel the first man to strike terror among the population. As early as 1935, there was an intensive police hunt for a man known as The Night Prowler, who was never found. In 1946, terror struck again but here, too, a culprit was never found.

The events, however, that took place on the night of Sunday, 6th March 1960, were to cause a wave of horror and fear to run through Jersey. I ought to say that at this stage, seven attacks of a sexual nature had already taken place on women and young children within the space of three years; two of them, indeed, in that year itself – one in January, the other in February. Publicity, however, had been minimal nor, as yet, had the regular C.I.D. become fully alarmed, primarily because of the seven, three had not been notified to the C.I.D. and the first attack had been listed as Grievous Bodily Harm. On Saturday, 30th November 1957, a 29-year-old nurse waiting for a bus in the Monte a l'Abbe area was attacked and severely injured by a man described as about forty, 5 feet 6 inches in height, with an 'Irish accent' and wearing a mask. She had been dragged into a field before fighting off her attacker and had to have several stitches in her wounds. On Saturday, 1st March 1958, a 20-year-old woman walking home from a bus stop near Augres Post Office, in the parish of Trinity was attacked by a man who tied a rope round her neck, dragged her into a field and then raped her. She described him as about 5 feet 6 inches tall, stockily built, with, significantly, a limp. The man had worn a scarf over the lower part of his face. On Saturday, 12th July 1958, in the lovely Rozelle district, a 31-year-old woman, again waiting or walking to a bus stop was attacked and raped by a man who put a rope round her neck, led her into a field where he tied her hands and feet. Again she described him as about 5 feet 6 inches and he also wore a scarf on his face.

The next *two* cases did not come to light, so far as the regular C.I.D. were concerned until 1961 when Detective-Superintendent Jack Manning of Scotland Yard was seconded to the island to help try to trap the sex maniac. In fact on Saturday, 29th August 1959, a man waiting in a field, pounced on a young girl walking home in the parish of Grouville, flung a rope round her neck, dragged her into a field and raped her. She thought he was about 5 feet 7 inches tall, with an 'Irish accent' and he had a scarf over his face. He also wore a rope or cord round his waist – which was the first time *this* had been mentioned.

On Saturday, 19th October 1959, a 28-year-old woman was dragged into a field in the parish of St Martin's. The assailant grabbed hold of her and assaulted her indecently but she was able to fight back successfully so that he quickly made off. She was able to give a pretty precise description of him – about 5 feet 6 inches tall, wearing a French beret and a raincoat with a piece of string or cord tied round his waist and wearing a mask. What she particularly noticed about him was 'a musty smell.'

One case that was reported to the C.I.D. was that of a $7\frac{1}{2}$-year-old schoolgirl, living at La Rocque who awoke on the night of Saturday, 9th January 1969 to find a strange man, who had apparently climbed in through the window, in her bedroom. The man wearing 'a macintosh' and had a mask over his face. The child was indecently assaulted in her bed.

On Sunday, 14th February 1960, a 12-year-old schoolboy, living in Grands Vaux one of the ripple of valleys running north to south that break up the interior of Jersey, was woken up by a man who had climbed in through a window who then tied a cord or rope round his neck and led him outside where he indecently assaulted him. In this case, the description was rather rough – the man had worn a plastic macintosh or raincoat and had 'spoken in a soft voice'. Unfortunately for the C.I.D., this case was not reported to them until much later when the scare had reached its height.

Trapping a will-o'-the-wisp criminal who can strike at any moment in any place he pleases demands all the resources, skill and perserverance of a high-trained C.I.D. force – and there are many in Jersey who find the present police system here unsatisfactory. The island, in their view, has a superfluidity of police forces, for it has *two*; and in the case of trapping Ted Paisnel, the view inclines to the belief that too many cooks do, indeed, spoil the broth.

The first force is known as The Honorary Police – on paper a body representing 200 volunteers; the second, the 135-man

42

States of Jersey regular, professional police. This latter force is uniformed and well-equipped with most of the paraphernalia of modern police forces – patrol cars, radio-cars, an up-to-date C.I.D. and so forth. To the newcomer to Jersey they are indistinguishable from policemen on the British mainland.

The Honorary Police spring from the peculiar history of the Channel Islands which, for centuries, were more or less allowed to rule themselves and have thus developed institutions very different from those in Britain. In 933, Jersey, along with the other Channel Islands, became part of the Duchy of Normandy, that great segment of land which the ferocious Northmen, or Vikings, had carved for themselves out of northern France. As the Duke of Normandy eventually became King of England – English history knows him as William the Conqueror – Jerseymen tend to regard Britain as belonging to them rather than the other way round. Today, for example, the loyal toast in Jersey is always given as, 'To the Queen – our Duke!'.

When Duke William assumed the Crown of England in 1066, Jersey, however, was not immediately annexed to that Crown but, instead, remained part of the Duchy of Normandy. Jersey paid its taxes to Normandy; its money was minted at Rouen and its Judges came from that city. Until the reign of King John, Jersey, strictly speaking, remained a fiefdom of the King of France. When John lost his Norman patrimony, however, Jersey did not go with the rest of Normandy, but remained a possession of the English Crown, although up until the Reformation it remained part of the diocese of Coutances, the spires of whose cathedral are visible on a clear day from the top of Mont Orgueil. In secular matters, however, the Channel Islands were found to be too remote to be comfortably incorporated into the administration of the British mainland as an ordinary English county; so Jersey was allowed to follow its own inclinations to such an extent that it evolved a constitution and body of customs entirely its own.

This had meant, in effect, that apart from displaying such pleasing idiosyncracies as speaking the Norman-French spoken by the Conqueror himself, much of the law of the island is based on the *Grand Coutumier de Normandie*. Old legal customs unheard of in England survive, including the *Clameur de Haro*. Any Jerseyman who feels he is suffering a serious wrong has only to shout aloud in the presence of witnesses, '*Haro! haro! haro! à l'aide mon Prince. On me fait tort* (Haro! haro! haro! –

43

aid me, my Prince, I am being wronged)' and the wrongdoer must desist until the dispute has been thrashed out in court.

The virtual rulers of Jersey became the twelve elected magistrates called Jurats who were subject only to the overriding authority of the Warden, the King's Representative. At weekly meetings they conducted all the business of Jersey, settling disputes, trying criminals and passing, where necessary, laws and regulations. These weekly meetings came to be called the Royal Court. Eventually the Jurats began summoning rectors and constables to advise them and the meetings grew into a body known as The States, a kind of local Parliament. Since 1948, however, the Jurats have been relegated to their original role as Judges only.

Another institution peculiar to Jersey (and the other Channel Islands) was the establishment of an Honorary Police Force. This consisted – and still consists – of twelve Constables, each representing the twelve parishes of Jersey – Grouville, St Brelade, St Clement, St Helier, St John, St Lawrence, St Martin, St Mary, St Ouen, St Peter, St Saviour and Trinity. These constables originally chaired parish assemblies and under them were *centeniers*, each of whom was responsible for one hundred families in his parish and *vingteniers*, each responsible for twenty. All were, and are, *elected* officials. In total, the Honorary Police Force now consists of 12 constables, 43 *centeniers* and 145 *vingteniers*. They are, basically, a volunteer force ready, in theory at least, to turn out at any time which, in practice, generally means at week-ends only. They are identifiable only by a pin-on brooch badge with the Jersey coat-of-arms and a card in their pockets. They are, in effect, merely a part-time police force, almost totally lacking professional training. They come from all walks of life; for instance, Mr C. A. Goodsman, the St Helier *centenier* who arrested and prosecuted my husband, is a Methodist lay preacher by profession.

For this is the extraordinary case in Jersey – the regular, professional police *have no powers of arrest !* All powers of arrest and prosecution are vested in the honorary police only. Outside the capital town of St Helier, the regular police do not even patrol a beat and only one parish – St Brelade – has so far allowed the professional police to set up a sub-station. In no other modern state in the world are the professional police, in effect, so hamstrung. Before an arrest can be made, a *centenier* must be called in.

44

It is a system, clearly presenting obvious weaknesses – although the strengths are also obvious. *Centeniers* and *vingteniers* tend to be a more integral part of their communities than the regular police of Britain, for instance. On the whole, they *ought* to know not only everyone in their parish but all the gossip of that parish. And intelligence of this kind, of course, is the basis of all police work, as I understand it. Yet it is a system that must give rise to a kind of paternalism; it is not easy for a *centenier* to believe the worst of a man or woman whom he has possibly gone to school with; whom he has possibly lived alongside for all his life. In practice, too, there are delays and hold-ups when the regular police, hard on the heels of a criminal, must wait for a *centenier* if they wish to secure an arrest.

Perhaps the greatest drawback in the present system, from the point of view of the professional police, is that, despite the establishment of a highly efficient '999' system on Jersey which, it is claimed, is even more efficient than Britain's, most islanders still telephone their *centeniers* in an emergency. Local *centeniers* first investigate inquiries; then, if they seem of a serious or complex nature – and then only – do they call in the regular police. The assaults of 29th August 1959 and 18th October, 1959 were reported to the Honorary Police only and local *centeniers*, after listening to the accounts, did not consider them serious enough and, in effect, did nothing more.

It was the events of Sunday, 6th March 1960, which were really to arouse a hue and cry in the island. These began at about 2 or 2.30 p.m. that day. It was a dull March day, just gone February and the residents of Jersey, particularly those living in Vallée des Vaux, were still in the grip of a winter *malaise*; in other words, boredom hung heavily over the valley. Idly, Mrs Stanley Boston who lives with her husband and 10-year-old son Eric in a pretty little villa in the lea of a *cotil* or steep hillside, stared out at the wide field opposite. She saw a man walking across it, going towards *L'Ecluse*, the big house owned by Brigadier Starling. He was dressed in a light blue pullover, dark trousers and he wore no hat. His hair was 'lightish-looking'. At the fairly considerable range between them, Mrs Boston was not able to make out the man's features.

At about 4 p.m. or thereabouts, she was pottering about in her front garden when a Rover car, No 18048, which she instantly recognized as the Brigadier's, came slowly down the valley road and came slowly round the bend just above the spot where the

Boston's house stands. Even a passing car, in the circumstances, was 'a big event – after all, there's not much to see here on a Sunday afternoon in March, it can be very miserable' as Mrs Boston puts it. So she took a good look. To her surprise, the driver was not the familiar figure of the Brigadier. Instead, it was a man with short-cropped or crew-cut hair – 'like a Hun's' – wearing a grey dufflecoat, the hood of which lay across the back of the seat (a coat which the police later identified as one stolen from a car only a short time previously in the same valley). The driver had the window down so she had a good look at his face. It was pale, but what she particularly noticed were the staring eyes. A little later, she went inside the house and remarked to her husband, 'The Brigadier isn't driving his car this evening'. It was quite unusual, really; and the Bostons puzzled a little, as people will when time is hanging heavily. 'Oh, it's probably some relative staying with him and he's lent him the car' observed her husband. And that, for the time being, was that.

That Sunday evening, as had become customary, an attractive 25-year-old girl called Joy Mellish who worked as an air hostess with the local airline visited her father in the Portelet Bay area of Jersey, which lies in the south-western parish of St Brelade, a few miles west of the town of St Helier. Twice a week, whenever her duties permitted, she visited him to make sure that he got a hot meal. Sunday was her normal visiting day and she usually caught the 9.45 bus back into St Helier. Normally, too, she took her dog along with her, 'just in case.'

That day, looking back, she considers three things to 'have gone wrong'. First, she could have driven herself up to see her father, for she had just bought herself a car. However, she was a rather inexperienced driver and did not feel like risking it. Second, she could – and should – have followed her normal practice and taken her dog with her. For some inexplicable reason, she chose not to. Third – and an event over which she had no control – she had 'a bit of a row with my father – oh, nothing important, we've just got too much of the same temperament'. This last had a fatal effect, for it meant that she missed her usual bus and had to stay at her father's house later than usual. In due course, she left to walk to the bus stop four minutes away.

Just as she turned right into the main Portelet Road – the bus stop was in sight now – she saw a Rover car draw up on the far side of the road. A voice hailed her, 'I'm going into town (St

46

Helier) can I give you a lift?' The driver added something – she can no longer remember the exact words – but they implied that he was a doctor and 'was going to pick up his wife'. On an impulse, she said 'yes' and got into the front seat beside the driver. He was wearing a cap *and* a duffle-coat and, in the dark, she could just dimly make out his profile. He spoke with a slight 'Irish accent' – or so it seemed to her. He wore gloves.

She first felt a sense of alarm when the man began to drive 'very fast, but very erratically'. In fact, she thought him 'a terrible driver', which increased her alarm. 'Irish accent' or not, too, he had obviously lived in Jersey a long time, if he were not, in fact, a real Jerseyman 'for no stranger could have driven in Jersey the way he did – he knew all the roads like the back of his hand.' Suddenly he turned the car into a field.

'What the hell do you think you're doing?' demanded Miss Mellish.

The driver said nothing. He simply got out, walked round the car, opened the door and asked her to get into the back seat. When she refused, he 'grabbed me and I tried to fight him off, but he was very strong.

'He pulled me out and tied my hands behind my back and the next thing I knew there was a rope around my neck. I was screaming my head off.' She now noticed, too, that the man was wearing a face mask, although she had not noticed him slipping it on. He then led her into the field and told her to lie down.

'He slapped me a few times and said he was going to kill me. He said he had killed before. The thing that struck me was that he was obviously experienced; he didn't waste any energy, he obviously knew exactly what he was doing. In other words, it wasn't a case of a drunken bungling sort of fool. As he seemed relatively elderly, I formed the impression that normally he was a perfectly respectable next-door neighbour type. Thinking about it afterwards, I felt perfectly convinced that he would kill the next time – or in the near future.'

He then raped her.

Afterwards he lifted her and began to carry her back to the car. He told her he would take her back to St Helier and asked her where she lived. She refused to tell him precisely, simply saying that she lived 'near West Park'. He said he would drop her there, but she didn't believe him. 'I knew I was in too great a mess – and it seemed obvious to me that he wasn't going to drive me into St Helier in that state.' At that moment, she really began to fear for her life. She was still tied up as he dumped her in the rear seat and she pretended to pass out. 'Luckily, although my hands were still tied behind my head, I felt confident that I could get them back over my head if I got the chance.'

With a grinding of gears, the man put the car into reverse and backed out of the field. Then he began to drive in the same fast, erratic fashion as earlier. Joy could think of no way out of her predicament except to lie there, pretending to have fainted, until they drove into an area with some street-lighting; the part of the island where the rape had actually taken place was near the airport and was unlighted countryside.

'I couldn't sit up – because the longer he thought I had passed out, it seemed to me, the better. I couldn't do anything, either, to attract the attention of two cars coming behind because I thought that if I tried, he would realize what I was trying to do and stop me.' But still lying slumped down quietly in the back seat, she was able to see some kind of street lighting ahead – probably cross-roads. The car slowed down a bit and she quietly slipped her tied hands over her head, prepared to leap out. She had noticed that the doors of the Rover swung open at the front – that is, with hinges at the rear – as with most pre-war cars and present-day London taxis. She realized that if she could just get a door open even the tiniest bit, the onrushing wind would do the rest for her and blow it wide open.

Gently she managed to grasp the door handle.

'I managed to get the car door open, when he turned round and realized that I intended to jump out. Then it all happened at once. He turned round and grabbed me – and this was when I saw his face clearly, full face. There were not only the street lights but as I opened the door, the interior car lights also went on.

'Then he sort of spun the car round, going to the left and I got my feet out and started to scream blue murder. Then, somehow or other, I managed to throw myself out of the car, even while it was still moving.'

Joy Mellish, in a dishevelled and distraught state ran across the road to a bungalow, even as the car driver began to reverse. There were two young people sitting in another car parked on the opposite side of the road and Joy yelled, 'Follow that car!' Unfortunately, as she found out later, they had just learned to drive; besides, it took them a little time to grasp what had happened; and, by then, of course, it was too late, although the young men gave chase. As for Joy herself, she stood there still screaming until people living nearby came out and found her. Both the police and her doctor were called and she made a signed statement to the police. The latter informed her that allegations similar to hers were not uncommon and said they would like to have further proof. They would pick her up in the morning at 9 o'clock and try and retrace the evening's car drive.

The following morning, the police called as promised and 'after a drive into the western part of the island and a considerable bit of reconnoitring, we eventually managed to find the field where I had been raped. I still don't know whether the police believed me or not at this stage, despite the medical evidence. But by enormous luck, there in the field they found my missing earring – a yellow pearl flat disc.'

Over the years, as the series of sex-crimes continued and police attempts to trap 'the sex-maniac' – as the newspapers described him – failed, the police came in for a considerable body of criticism. Rumours began to abound, the most persistent of which was that the fiend was the son of some high-up person on the island whose name was being deliberately kept secret. Joy, for example, says that when it became known that she had seen her attacker full-face, she was accused, on various occasions and by various people, of having been 'paid to keep my mouth shut'.

Mr and Mrs Stanley Boston are not without strong criticism of the island police, either. They claim that they made no attempt to interview people in Vallée des Vaux who might have witnessed the theft of the Brigadier's Rover. Mrs Boston herself saw the car again the next morning, 7th March, while she was taking her son to school. This was at the far end of the valley, on a hill, and she noticed it parked very untidily outside a telephone booth, its wheels out 'and very dirty-looking'. She remarked to Eric, 'Look at the car! It seems very strange, out here at this hour of the morning and looking like that!' However, she thought no more about it. The car itself then appears to have been moved – Mrs Boston believes the thief was probably in the phone booth making a call – for the police eventually picked it up at another place in Grands Vaux. In the local evening paper next day, 8th March, she read that the car had been 'borrowed' and that police presumed it had been used in an assault on a young lady who had been offered a lift. She admits, however, that she made no effort to volunteer her information to the police herself, although she could clearly remember the face of the man she had seen driving the car on Sunday – 'the very pale skin and those very blue, staring, large, cold eyes and this sandy, gingerish hair'.

The Bostons quickly sank back into the ordinary routine of their lives, in the absence of police activity in their valley under no real pressure to connect the man Mrs Boston had seen driving the car on the Sunday afternoon with the assailant of the air hostess; the episode, as it ordinarily does with people who have no direct interest, sinking into the recesses of their minds, and finally being lost out of sight. It was a memory that would have probably stayed out of sight for good had it not been for an extraordinary incident that occurred to them, just a little over six months later; late on Saturday, 24th September, to be precise.

Towards midnight, husband and wife heard a loud bump on the roof of their bungalow. Just prior to this, Mrs Boston and her boy Eric, had been working in the kitchen. The kitchen is arranged in such a way that the major light in the room comes through a fanlight in the ceiling which is not covered with any kind of curtaining. This, of course, means that any intruder trespassing in that part of their garden lying on top of the small cliff or *cotil*, could have a clear view of their movements.

The loud bump, as though someone had been peering over the *cotil* and had lost his balance and fallen over, was followed by a series of smaller bumps and noises, rising in crescendo to a final loud crash at the back of the bungalow. Mr Boston, although in late middle age, grabbed a torch and, followed by his wife, dashed outside. Crouched down between the rock face and the back of the bungalow in a space no more than two or three yards wide, was a figure.

'What the hell's going on here?' demanded Mr Boston loudly. He ordered the fellow to come out and straightening up, the man came forward.

He presented a strange sight. He was dressed in a faded blue pullover or sweater – a round-neck affair – and he was wearing dark navy or navy-blue serge trousers rather like a policeman's. He was wearing no shoes but had the trousers' ends tucked into his socks. His clothing was saturated from the knees down – seemingly from the damp grass – and he was covered in grass seeds and other similar debris. His socks seemed too big for him for 'some two inches of surplus sock were flapping about on his feet'.

'What's going on here?' demanded Mr Boston again.

In a 'peculiar kind of voice', the strange apparition answered, 'We're just having a bit of fun.'

'Who's *we* ?' asked Mr Boston.

'Oh, there's two more up the garden,' said the intruder.

Determined to eject them, too, Mr Boston started off up the steep slope to the top of the escarpment. He had got about half-way up the slope when he suddenly heard a commotion from below and turned back at once. He got down in time to find his wife remonstrating at the door with the intruder. It seems that almost as soon as Mr Boston started up the garden and Mrs Boston and her son had gone inside the house again, the intruder had begun fumbling with the door handle, in an obvious attempt to open it. At once Mrs Boston had gone to the door and flung it wide open. The light had fallen full on the man and she could see his face clearly. She had a feeling that it was familiar, but did not have time to place it immediately.

'What do you want ?' she demanded.

The man stood there, a half-crazed look in his very wide, staring, very cold, Nordic-type face, which at that date, was quite bony. His hair was light-coloured and grizzled or crew-cut. He stared blankly for a moment, then said,

'You wouldn't understand.'

'What are you doing – dressed like that ?' she demanded again, but he gave no answer. Then Mr Boston arrived at the door and grabbing the man by the arm, took him to the front gate and then led him down the road. Mr Boston made further efforts to communicate with him, but could get no sense out of him and after instructing him how to reach St Helier, returned to his house. Then he decided to telephone the police and went next door and did so. The two police motorcyclists arrived in double-quick time, one of whom set about helping Mr Boston to search the rest of the gardens for any sign of the intruder's companions. None was found – although next day, an old builder's shovel with a piece of cement sticking to it, was found on the top of the cliff; a clue which nobody, it appears, ever followed up. Satisfied that there was nobody else around, Mr Boston explained that the man had not been wearing boots or shoes and while the policeman was searching the garden with his torch, a police car rolled up. In it were two police constables and in the back seat, the strange intruder.

'The two policemen were chatting with him and asking him where his shoes were and so on,' says Mr Boston. 'Questions like, 'What are you doing like this?' and that sort.' Mr Boston asked one of the constables where they had found him and he answered, 'Oh, down in the Valley, seated in a car'. Then the police drove off, taking the man with them.

The Bostons expected to be closely questioned by the police and asked to sign statements, but day followed day and no one came near them. Some weeks later, while out on business for his firm, Mr Boston bumped into the officer whose men had come to their assistance on that particular night.

'What was the outcome of that affair?' asked Mr Boston.

'Oh, he was only a bloke who got lost,' answered the policeman.

'That's funny,' replied Mr Boston, 'I've never seen a chap get lost like that before – and in his stocking feet.'

'Well, that's what happened,' shrugged the officer and went off.

By this time, other serious sex attacks had taken place on the island and appeals for information that might help the police had been published in the local newspaper. The Bostons made no effort to raise the matter of their intruder, partly on the grounds that 'one doesn't like getting mixed up in these kind of cases', but more importantly because they were conscious that the police *knew* all about him already.

Only when, eleven years after the events of that year, had my husband been put on trial for a series of sex offences, did the story of these two episodes really come to light. Mrs Boston, shown photographs of my husband taken both recently and at the time of the attack on the air hostess, was able to identify him as the man wearing the duffle-coat whom she had seen driving the Brigadier's car on the afternoon of Sunday, 6th March 1960, and also as the 'strange intruder' who had so startled both her husband and herself six months later. In court, she was able to pick him out, although she made the point that in the intervening years he had changed to some degree; in particular, he now wore his hair considerably longer and it was greased down so that it was both smoother and slightly darker but she had no doubt but that it was Ted Paisnel.

Questions that have raised considerable comment on the island are how Ted Paisnel, if it were really he who was picked up by the police that night, was 1) set free, 2) never suspected, 3) not interrogated properly. The explanation, as I understand it, is bizarre in the extreme. One of the two constables who picked him up, to begin with, is no longer with the States of Jersey police. Some two months after this episode the man simply disappeared and is now believed to be living in England although his wife has obtained a divorce on the ground of his presumed death. It seems that he knew my husband very well, having undertaken building work for him during his spare time. The implication of this is that knowing only the Jekyll side of my husband's character, the officer could not believe that Ted was involved in anything except an innocent escapade, and considered him slightly drunk. Who the second constable was has never been satisfactorily established.

Whatever the explanation, one thing is certain: the uniformed officers made no report of the incident or, if it *were* properly logged, details of the incident were never passed to the C.I.D. The whole story was to lie unrevealed until a day, eleven years later, when Detectives Marsh and Lang, desperately hunting for evidence that would convince a court that Ted Paisnel was the beast who had terrorized Jersey for years, decided to drive out to where everything connected with the case seemed to start from – to Vallée des Vaux.

FOUR

MARRIAGE TO TED

I still find it difficult to accept, in any emotional sense, that the man I married should have been such a monster although rationally, of course, I have no alternative but to accept the strong body of evidence against him that ultimately led to his conviction in court. The phrase 'Jekyll and Hyde' had never meant much to me; I had never realized how easy it is to be deluded by someone who, to all intents and purposes, is suffering from schizophrenia – although I must accept the expert opinion of the psychiatrist who examined Ted before his trial and pronounced him fit to plead.

A full perspective on the inherent drama of the Paisnel case cannot be obtained, I believe, unless the domestic background against which the more sordid aspects of the case were played out, is explained. In most respects, I believe, they serve only to heighten the incredible and bizarre nature of Ted Paisnel's life and of his extraordinary and abhorrent career.

By birth I am a Londoner. My father was a hard-working taxi-driver who was eventually obliged to give up his job as a result of a serious accident. My parents did their best for me and had some small ambitions as I showed talent, as a child, as a dancer. Although there was never a lot of money to spare, both my mother and father saw that I attended a good dancing school, followed by ballet classes. I performed in cabaret and at charity functions and had a very enjoyable and successful career until the outbreak of war. I spent the war years in the W.A.A.F.

I went back to dancing after the war and eventually became a teacher of ballroom dancing, as well as taking classes in ballet. I also got married – to a man who was a reader in the printing department of a Fleet Street newspaper. The marriage was happy at first but when our daughter was born I longed to get away from the 'hot house' atmosphere of the dancing world, to the lovely island of Jersey with its more natural beauty in which to bring up a family.

Following his accident, my father cast around for another way of earning a living. He and my mother had spent quite a few holidays on Jersey and had come to love it, so my father hit on the idea of buying a large old house and turning it into a guest house. It was run initially as a place for vegetarians. I had met some vegetarian friends when I was about sixteen; I was at an age then when I was looking around as most young people do, for some belief or philosophy to adhere to and meeting some other young people who were connected with the Oxford Group Movement and Quakers and who were vegetarians, I quickly became converted to the idea of food reform. In due course both my parents were also converted.

I came over several times to help run the guest house. I had hoped that my husband would feel the same way about Jersey as I did – although a Londoner, I love the countryside and the kind of life that permits a person to breathe fresh air and enjoy the beauties of nature. I felt that in an island with such natural beauty, the harmony of our surroundings would induce a new atmosphere in our marriage. My husband did not like the island, however, and yearned to get back to his beloved London. Our separation became final and I obtained a divorce on the grounds of desertion. With my two children, I settled down to a new life.

As those things often do happen, the transformation from guest house to childrens home came about more or less by accident. The vegetarian group with which we were associated in England closed down its small children's home and we were asked if we could accommodate the three children they had left, on a temporary basis. My parents were happy to agree, and we looked around for a more suitable house where we could take some of the island's more necessitous children.

Jersey had at that time no elaborate system of child care such as exists on the British mainland. From time to time my parents and I read pathetic advertisements in the local press advertising children for adoption. This seemed such a worthy and, indeed, *necessary* social work that my parents decided to turn our house into a proper house for foster children. We applied to the States for a licence to run such a home and we were granted it. Out quota was fourteen children though today it is twenty. In the first few months, I decided to start a nursery school, with the intention of helping out financially, and for a short while we had these little toddlers arriving daily at the house. But as more and more orphans or illegitimate children or children simply needing

55

care because of the death of one parent or a broken marriage arrived, it became necessary to close down the nursery school.

Then we suffered a bitter blow. In May 1958, my father, Sidney died. It proved almost a complete disaster because he was such a marvellous help to us and the children. Now there was just my mother and I and a staff nurse to carry out the work. We had very little money and to eke it out, the three of us stitched and sewed clothes for the children, for we could not afford to buy them any, and all three of us took our turn to scrub the floors and so on. It was a life of considerable hardship but never monotonous, relieved as it was by the sense of dedication we felt for our task.

Somehow or other we got through the months of summer and autumn but that first Christmas without my father presented a bleak prospect. One is often astonished, however, at the innate kindness and concern of people. One day a letter appeared in the local newspaper drawing attention to our plight. I have not kept the text but it ran along the lines 'Do people realize that there are two lone women trying to cope with all those children in the island – two dedicated women short both of money and help?'. The result of this well-wisher's letter was a marvellous response. We were simply inundated with help and gifts. Parties were held to raise funds for us and farmers drove up daily with cauliflowers or other vegetables as gifts for the home. There were jumble sales. All over the parish, it was the same: 'What are you doing to make it a really good Christmas for the necessitous children.' The sheer kindness, compassion and thoughtfulness of people, once our plight had been brought to their notice, were remarkable.

On Christmas Eve some carol singers from St Saviour's Mental Hospital were going around their parish, which is next to ours, St Martin, visiting hotels and pubs with a collecting box, rattling it gaily. They were collecting funds for us. In due course, they went into the lounge bar of the Longueville Manor Hotel. Ted happened to be sitting there. He was alone and he was in a very depressed state.

His depression, I have since learned, was due to the fact that he had recently lost his girl friend. When I married Ted Paisnel I had absolutely no idea of the extent of his philandering. Only since his trial and conviction, has the whole extraordinary nature of this become known to me.

I shall not reveal the girl's name, but it seems that she and Ted were, 'living together'. Ted seems to have been genuinely fond

56

of her and, so I understand, proposed marriage to her. For some reason of which I am unaware but can make a reasonable guess at, she decided to jilt Ted and marry another suitor.

That Christmas Eve of 1958 Ted Paisnel, as was frequently his fate throughout his life, was on his own when the St Saviour's carol singers jingled their collecting tin in front of him. He asked what they were collecting for and they told him. They also explained that the children's home was a strictly vegetarian home. As he himself was tinkering with diets and herbalist remedies, he remarked, 'That's interesting'. Shortly after the war, with its privation and hunger, he had got very fat and then when he went to Wales, following his first marriage, as the saying goes, 'he blew himself out'. He has told me that he then met a monk who put him on a diet of herbs and other vegetarian dishes which helped him to get back to normal size.

The upshot was that Ted asked if he could join the carol singers and help out in whatever way he could. One can put whatever interpretation one likes upon the offer – that he was simply bored and wanted something to do; that the word 'children' struck a responsive chord in the evil compartments of his mind; or, as I prefer to think, that when in his Jekyll moods, there was a lot of good in him. Can anybody be wholly evil ? Or, as many others have suggested, was it all part of the *alter ego* Ted Paisnel was deliberately creating – the image of a kind, good cheery man who would not hurt a fly ? As I shall explain later, Ted was a marvellous actor and mimic. There can be no doubt, either, that his mind worked in the most tortuous, devious ways. Was he full of guile and cunning ? What his real interest was in coming to the children's home that Christmas Eve we shall, I suppose, never know.

Anyhow, he turned up with the jolly party which arrived at the Home that Christmas Eve and piled up a considerable amount of money on the table in the sitting room. I cannot say that I gave him anything more than a passing glance or two – he was just one of the men, so far as I was concerned. He only stepped out of the crowd, so to speak, when at the end of the evening, he lingered behind after the others had gone and we all had a conversation together.

'Look!' he told me, 'you seem to need help – just two women and temporary staff trying to run this big place and look after these children. Can I help in any way ?'

He could see that we were reluctant, so he pressed, 'I'm a

builder, you see and I'm sure I could help in several ways. Is there anything you'd like me to do as regards maintaining the house? It seems to be getting a bit dilapidated in places. The roof and the other things need attention.'

'Well, yes – ' I began.

'I won't charge you anything,' he interrupted, 'beyond the cost of the materials.'

'After Christmas, I'm sure you could help' I said. 'You must realize that in a place like this we get a lot of 'do-gooders' coming up and offering to help us. Some of them are genuine and some are not. So we have to be a little careful and we don't usually jump at a first offer like that.'

'I understand,' he replied.

'But if you still feel the same after Christmas, do come up and we'd be happy to have your help.'

This, it appeared, was not quite what he had in mind – he must have been terribly lonely and depressed.

'But is there nothing I can do *right now*! – this Christmas!'

In fact, there was. Every other year my father had dressed up in a Father Christmas outfit to hand our presents to the children. Now that he was dead, we had a problem.

'Actually, there is something you could do. We haven't got a Father Christmas to put on the red coat and give the toys out in the afternoon.'

'Why, I'd love to do that!' said Ted.

True to his word, he was up at the home bright and early the next morning, Christmas Day. There are really no words to describe the extraordinary rapport Ted Paisnel could establish with children. One might now consider that there was something sinister about it but when one watched him playing so naturally with them, tossing them into the air and catching them; playing all sorts of games with them; listening to their squeals of delight and cries of 'Uncle Ted' this and 'Uncle Ted' that, one could only see him as the kindest and gentlest of men. He was quite marvellous. When people now say to me, 'But you must have suspected Ted?', I can only reply that they had never seen him the way I had. The idea that a man who could captivate innocent young children in this way; who could, not to put too fine a point on it, make them *love* him – that idea that a man with such a capacity for bestowing love on *them*, could harm a hair of an innocent child's head, still seems fantastic to me.

Ted hung around the home for the rest of the holiday; on one occasion, I remember, he brought his mother up as well. I was very impressed with him. He was kind, gentle, full of fun. He never tired of amusing the children in some way or other and when he wasn't in the centre of some circle of children, squealing with delight, he was busy mending and fixing things for us. Among the other chores he carried out was a thorough cleansing of the drains. I also discovered that he was a very well-read man. A day or two after Christmas, I found him in our library. He and I chatted a bit about various vegetarian diets and he picked out some books on the subject. But I also noticed that he was attracted towards serious subjects. He began scanning one of our books on the history of the Bible and he relaxed with one or two books on astrology. The general impression I had at this stage was of a very kind, considerate man, with a wonderful sense of humour, extremely fond of children and anxious to help those who needed it (he was always for the underdog) and a man with a cultivated mind; he seemed to be able to talk on any subject, and talk very interestingly. He also spoke well.

It would be entirely wrong to say that Ted and I fell madly in love with each other just like that! We were both mature people, long past the time when a pretty face or a broad pair of shoulders can create a tumult of one's feelings. Both of us had a broken marriage behind us. Neither of us was capable of being swayed by fanciful notions of romance. But we both did need someone to care for and be cared by. And, initially, we both seemed to be most compatible.

Ted's first marriage had been to a Welsh girl, daughter of an accountant in Llanelly in Carmarthenshire, South Wales. Her name was Joan Davies and thus she became Joan Paisnel, the significance of which I shall duly explain. Both his wives, therefore, bore the name Joan Paisnel. They were married on St Valentine's Day, 14th February 1950 and eventually had one child, a little girl called Teri, short for Terinne.

The date, of course, I have since learned, has a special significance for witches, being associated with the Feast of Lupercal or the God Pan – the Horned God. Not the least remarkable aspect of Ted Paisnel's infamous life is that his daughter by this marriage is also susceptible to witchcraft. And this despite the fact that they never got to know each other until after his arrest in July 1971 when she wrote to him in prison and then came across to St Helier to see him. I was astonished at her appearance. She has waist-length dark-red hair and she wore an ankle-length black cape, with knee-high black boots with metal crosses hanging from them and a large studded cross on her chest. She told reporters that she was fascinated by witchcraft and that she had attended a coven. She insisted that she had a genuine interest in it and was not simply fascinated by the idea of sex that seemed to accompany some of the ceremonies. 'I think there is nothing more disgusting than copulating on a gravestone,' she has been reported in a newspaper as saying. She had, she insisted, once refused to attend a coven because she knew that 'it was arranged only for people to have sex'. But she believed in the power of black magic and in devil worship and wore the studded cross when she went to see Ted in gaol because, as she explained, she was 'in fear that in some way black magic might affect me'. She seemed to believe that Ted had begun innocently enough with white magic and had then been drawn, willy-nilly, into working the Left Hand Path, that is practising the black side of magic.

This kind of thing, of course, was about the last thing that could possibly have crossed my mind in those first few weeks and months after I first met Ted. All I saw was a man who was interested in the things that I was interested in and who was coming out the other side of a broken marriage. To begin with, the idea that I might marry him never even crossed my mind. Yet I should make it clear that Ted *was* an attractive man. As I was later to discover, he had little difficulty attracting women, which makes the kind of crimes he committed all the more bizarre.

Our romance began very casually. It was Ted's idea that he and I ought to take the children out for a picnic in the woods or down to the beach somewhere. So he would call up at the Home and drive a small party of us out in my mother's van – at this stage, I was myself still unable to drive. I found his driving abilities rather surprising, for he seemed so capable in every other respect. But he was an extremely bad driver – slow, insistent on hugging the centre of the road, however many cars piled up behind and inclined to crash the gears. One had the feeling that any car he happened to own would need a new gear box every month or so.

After we were married, I once asked him, 'Have you ever had a driving lesson ?'

'Oh, no,' he replied cheerily, 'they have us a driving licence during the war.'

'Who did ?' I asked.

'The Germans. I practised with tractors and just acquired a licence!' By this time, after I had seen the other, violent side of his nature, he made no attempt to hide his annoyance with other road users. He would lose his temper on the road, use bad language and give a rude sign if anybody hooted at him. And the point was, *he* was always in the wrong! But one good thing, once I had learned to drive, he always insisted that I take the wheel and he was quite content to be a passenger.

In those early days, however, Ted showed me only his good side; and gradually the bonds between us grew closer and warmer. He told me a lot about himself and gradually the picture of a lonely, even tortured little boy who grew into a lonely, tortured young man began to emerge. Only later, after our marriage, would the full picture emerge, but I learned enough at that time to engage my sympathies.

He was devoted to his mother – I believe he and his mother loved each other dearly, although later they used to have terrible rows together. I believe, however, she had a considerable influence over him all the time she lived and that possibly she was responsible for introducing him to white witchcraft. Later, my mother-in-law would talk openly about witchcraft and about how curses had been put on certain people in Jersey; there was one family, in particular that had a curse put on it three generations ago that no girl child would survive to adulthood; of the three girl children of this generation, all have now died, apparently of a brain tumour, the last dying in 1970. Both Ted and my mother-in-law appeared to be convinced that black magic was responsible; he later told me that one whole family, once very well-known in Jersey, had died out completely because of a black magic curse. Had I known what lay ahead of me with this kind of talk, I have little doubt but that I would not have married Ted Paisnel.

He seemed to me, even in those first days of our acquaintance-ship, to have a mild persecution complex. His home, it appeared, was not altogether a happy one. His father, Emile Paisnel, although a hard-working and respectable farmer, from a family who claimed to have lived on the island since the thirteenth or fourteenth centuries, seems to have been a man who in his young days found it difficult to control his temper. After a few sessions in some local hostelry, his violence would explode within the family circle and the boy Ted would have to take the brunt. I do not think Ted had much love for his father in those days; indeed, the word 'hate' might not be too strong a word to use in connection with their relationship.

According to Ted, he was blamed for everything that went wrong, – either at home or at school. Ted was the eldest of the four children in the family and whenever any of them did anything wrong, Ted got the hiding for it. He went to school at St Brelade's School at St Aubin, then moved on to St Lawrence School later. He was a hopeless pupil, apathetic and uninterested and constantly playing truant. As at home, he was blamed for every misdemeanour. Only when he went to Trinity School where he came under the supervision of an inspiring teacher called Mrs Garvin, did his attitude towards schooling and learning change. She, it seems, worked miracles with him. Whatever academic abilities Ted now possesses, he owed to her, as he has frequently said himself.

He was a lonely boy, with no real capacity for making friends among his fellows. I gather he made only three close male friends during his life, but unfortunately all three died relatively young. The picture I have of him as a boy is of a lonely child, with a feeling of persecution slowly developing inside him. One, however, who found compensation, when he began playing truant, in learning to understand and love nature. In due course, he was to simply astonish me with his almost uncanny knowledge of rustic lore; with his profound knowledge of birds, animals, fish. Even as a boy, he learned to catch trout by the old method of tickling them. He spent hour after happy hour wandering around the valleys of Jersey, studying birds, animals, fish, learning about nature in a way that could never be explored in books. He appeared to develop extraordinary powers over animals – later the police would find that even the fiercest dog would turn into a whimpering, docile creature in his presence. Guard-dogs were useless as a method of preventing him entering a house in the silence of the night; he simply slipped past them like a ghost. Shortly before his arrest, at Easter 1970, he was caught by a man gazing through his window late at night. The man had a large and fierce Alsatian and immediately ran outside to tackle the peeping tom. All the intruder said – and in an 'Irish accent' at that, was 'I'm not doing anything wrong, sir.' Then he simply bolted, clearing a six foot fence before going over this *cotil* and rolling down the hillside – the most astonishing and perplexing feature of the whole business being that the Alsatian never even moved! Later, when Detectives Shutler, Marsh and Lang were calling on houses making inquiries following Ted's arrest, they were amazed at the way guard-dogs who had allowed Ted to enter the premises without as much as a whimper, 'went' for them.

I formed the impression that Ted became a master of wood-craft and nature lore in a similar fashion to a Red Indian. Certainly, it was during these solitary rambles, made as often by night as by day, that Ted came to know the valleys and fields of Jersey, particularly the eastern end of it, so well that he was able to flit as stealthily as shadow about the countryside when the police hunt for him was at its hottest. I have said he rambled a lot at night. He told me that while he was still quite young, his mother would tuck all the children into their beds fairly early on a summer evening so that she could join their father in the fields helping with the work. The moment her back was turned, young Ted would quietly slip out through a window and hurry off on his rambles, often not returning until 3 or 4 a.m. It was the beginning of a habit that he was to continue for the rest of his years of freedom.

He had an extraordinary war and it is, perhaps, only another of the fantastic aspects of Ted Paisnel's extraordinary character that he emerged from it as a kind of minor Robin Hood figure. Some people have suggested to me that he was a collaborator with the Germans, but from the respect in which he was held up until his arrest and from other things I have heard, he was given, as most Channel Islanders were, no option. It was either do as the Germans ordered or else. Ted, able to turn his hand to anything – he has, after all, been a blacksmith, quarryman, cobbler, miner, farmer and builder during his career – was forced to work as a cobbler for the Germans, mending the shoes of prisoners-of-war whom the Germans employed to dig the elaborate underground system of fortifications that were erected on Jersey. At that, he neglected no opportunity to help his fellow islanders. He constantly stole food from the Germans and distributed it among the most needy families. He stole lengths of hosepipe from them and turned the bits into bicycle tyres for the children. He even tried to steal shoes and distribute them among people in need. This time, however, the Germans caught him. He was jailed for a month. It was during this time, or so I understand, that he was maltreated a bit by the Germans, one of the guards slamming a rifle butt into his stomach and making him ill.

For a long time he simply refused to talk about the German

occupation, although I was quite interested in the subject. It was several years later before he would say anything more than, 'Oh, some horrible things happened then, you'd never believe them.' Then he told me a quite ghastly story. If true, I have the feeling that it might go a long way towards an explanation of why he was able to be so cruel himself later on.

He told me that the Germans imported large numbers of Russian women who had been captured on the Eastern Front, for the use of troops stationed on Jersey. These poor women were constantly giving birth to babies who were, of course, not allowed to live. According to Ted, he was pressed into service as a kind of midwife-extraordinary. The picture he painted was of rows of these poor Russian women, lying on the cold cement floor of what I gathered was a disused aircraft hangar, giving birth under the most appalling conditions. Both women and infants – certainly the latter, – invariably succumbed, or were helped to succumb. It is a terrible story and alas, I have no way of knowing whether it is true or not. Knowing his *penchant* for horror stories, it could well be a figment of his imagination. And yet he told the story with such reluctance that I must say he fully convinced me. It was not something he really wanted to boast about, the way people delight in capping each other's wartime bomb escapes; or, indeed, even to discuss.

It was during the war that Ted formed his first semi-permanent liaison with a woman. He was only eighteen at the time and she was a married woman aged about twenty-two or three originally from England. On the outbreak of war, her Jersey husband joined the French Army and, of course, was caught up in the debacle of May 1940; he did not, therefore, return to the island until the war was ended. At some indeterminate time, she and Ted became lovers and she eventually moved to Ted's home, Maison du Soleil, where she gave birth to a little girl. This woman has said that she would have starved, as many other people would have done, had it not been for Ted risking his neck and stealing food from the Germans. When the child was three, however, it took ill from bronchial pneumonia and died. Ted buried the little corpse in the Paisnel family grave and appeared inconsolable.

At some time, they both set up on their own in a little white stone cottage in Grands Vaux, the valley adjoining Vallée des Vaux. It was, apart from the death of the child and Ted's references to the Paisnel family curse of which I was to hear so much in due course, an extremely happy liaison. This woman has said that Ted is the 'only man I've ever loved or will love. I found him a perfect lover and there was absolutely nothing kinky or odd about the way he made love. We found ourselves totally compatible'. This idyllic relationship came to an abrupt end when her husband returned to the island after the Liberation. As she put it, 'There was a terrible emotional tug-of-war', but in the end she elected to fulfil her duty and return to her husband. Ted, I understand, was terribly broken up by it all and left the island for a time for France in an effort to forget. To this day, all three have remained close friends and Ted and her legitimate son, eventually became great friends, too; Ted often taking the boy fishing and showing him how to tickle trout.

On his return from France, he met Joan. Joan had come across to Jersey, I think about 1947, on a working holiday, picking tomatoes. She first got to know Malcolm, Ted's younger brother and for a while she and Malcolm went around together. Then Malcolm met another girl and decided to marry her. Ted, however, seems to have been captivated by Joan from the beginning and continued to write to her when she had returned to Wales. She wrote back asking if she could come to Boulivot des Bas for another working holiday and on 24th June 1949 she arrived in Jersey again. Ted went out to meet her at the airport and brought her to Maison du Soleil. She spent the holiday picking and packing tomatoes and then went back to Wales. By this stage, she and Ted had reached an understanding and then at Christmas that year Ted went over to Llanelly to meet her parents. They were married the following February.

Ted asked his parents for some rooms at Maison du Soleil and he was told 'Take what you like'. So, with the help of some French builders, he made a house for himself alongside the main part of Maison du Soleil – a flat consisting of bedroom, bathroom, lounge and kitchen. They settled down to live there, and Ted began working on the farm. However, he suffered from hayfever and this made if often difficult for him.

The marriage began to run on to the rocks within the first year. From all that I can gather, it was not really Ted's fault, or, at least, only partly his fault. She loved the excitement of dance-halls, film shows, pubs and so on and she found life down on the farm in a remote part of Grouville parish far from ideal. They went back to Wales and it was then that Joan announced that she was not returning to Jersey. Ted was obviously anxious to rescue the marriage and, I gather, got himself a job in Wales for a while. He returned to Jersey in the summer of 1951 and told his parents that he was 'packing up my home here, as I wish to keep my wife happy.'

He never told me much about his affairs during this period. I gather that he knocked about quite a bit, moving from one job to another. Finally he became a coal-miner and went down the pits in South Wales. He was badly injured in an accident in the pits. A pit prop went through his mouth and knocked out all his teeth. Sometimes he used to limp a bit and he always blamed this on his 'accident' – I never knew whether it was a genuine limp or not. His daughter Terrine, was born in April, 1953, but within two months he was back in Jersey and the marriage was in ruins. His mother told me that when he returned he was a 'very sick man' and the doctor had to call every day for the first week he was home. He explained that his wife was too fond of a 'a good time' and that he had decided to refurnish his home and remain permanently on Jersey. Shortly after this, when he was working in Manchester, he met an English girl who was in the process of divorcing her husband. Later she went to live at Boulivot. Three years after his separation from his first wife, Ted divorced her on the grounds of desertion. He and the English girl continued to live together until she met another man, and as I have related before, jilted Ted. I, therefore, more or less met him on the rebound.

In those first days of our courtship, I found Ted most compatible. He never showed any signs of aggression with me. I never, at any time, had to fend him off.

His attitude towards me, indeed, was extremely respectful and worshipful. He told people that he was proud to have captured a 'goddess' from London and seemed to put me on a pedestal rather than treat me as a woman of real flesh and blood with human feelings.

Later he was to call me 'Puritan Joan', a term that had once been applied to St Joan of Arc. The significance of this I shall come to in due course.

He seemed fascinated that although a 'town girl' I could find joy in practical hard work, child-care and helping him to build the house, for example, polishing and finishing the beautiful interior granite walls; that I swam from April to October in the sea round the island, and up to last year danced by request at various public gatherings a very energetic Mexican hat dance, backed by twelve other energetic ladies from a local social club. These things seemed to delight him, and he seemed proud – not at all the sort of husband who would shatter my life with scandal and horror.

Since his arrest, it has also been suggested to me by many people that one of Ted's reasons for marrying me was to gain himself a kind of 'respectability'. If, as is suspected, he began his series of sex-attacks before he even met me, then the suggestion does make sense to some extent. Certainly, his association, via me, with the children's home could only have redounded to his credit. Nor is it likely that people would suspect a man so closely identified with children in a very laudable capacity. These are only speculations, however; Ted has never admitted me to his innermost thoughts in this regard. So far as I knew at the time, he wanted to marry me because he wanted a wife and we found each other compatible.

I don't suppose I have ever sorted out properly my own reasons for marrying *him*. Certainly, despite my divorce, I had not lost faith in the institution of marriage and was only too anxious to try again. I believed that I had all the necessary qualifications for providing a good home for a man and making him very happy. It is true, of course, that when the subject of marriage arose between Ted and me, that I was not altogether thinking of the benefits such a union would have for me personally. I was too deeply immersed in the work being done by the home, not to take into account any advantages a marriage with him might bring. We desperately needed a man about the place; a sort of house-father. I knew he lacked polish at times, but so has a rough diamond. I am not snobbish and judge people by the values they show me. Kindness to others I consider very important, and Ted certainly showed that to me and everyone else he met. And then he had these premises at Maison du Soleil which we both considered – that is, Ted and me – might provide a very useful annexe for the main Home. The idea was that some of the kiddies who had no parents might be lodged there. One of the most heart-rending sights so far as I was concerned, was the way our little kiddies who had no parents at all used to have to stand aside and watch the others, who had at least one parent to visit them, go out and kiss the parent and receive presents. Ted and I discussed this aspect and he was very enthusiastic, showing every understanding.

In those few months before our marriage, things could not

have been more pleasant. Ted seemed to be capable of enjoying a certain degree of gracious living, a relic of his days in France and in Manchester and he loved taking me and my two children out and dining and wining us very well. He impressed me, of course, with his extraordinary range of knowledge – I found it almost impossible to believe that he had received no formal schooling beyond the age of 14. He could discuss history, philosophy, poetry, as well as subjects such as hypnotism. I know he read a lot about hypnotism, but whether he ever developed a capacity to hypnotize people or not, I cannot say. My daughter, nine-years-old, absolutely adored him – a very important consideration with me when he eventually got round to proposing. As for my son – his reaction to Ted was quite remarkable. Normally, he was a little boy who wouldn't go near a stranger attached only to my father, and it took a lot of coaxing to get him to sit on the knee of anybody he didn't know well. He was only about $2\frac{1}{2}$ at this time. But the first time he saw Ted, he went to him as though he had known him all his life – and right away climbed up his knee. To me, in my naivete, it seemed a wonderful sign; I believed, as I suppose most people must do, that anybody who had such a compelling power over little children could only be the epitome of goodness.

Yet the extraordinary thing about the whole affair is that when I went for the first time to Maison du Soleil (which, significantly, means The House of the Sun) a dark shadow seemed to fall across me. I looked around at this brooding, dark-grey stone house, with its shabby outhouses and its stacks of untidy, derelict rubbish of all kinds littered about everywhere and I can remember even now the terrible feeling of something oppressive, something not quite right, about it all. I find it very difficult to describe the feeling exactly, particularly because my memories are now distorted to some extent by what I now know. Yet the fact was – and I can still distinctly remember the chill I felt when Ted first brought me here – that I did shudder at my first sight of Maison du Soleil.

Ted assured me that he would make our quarters beautiful and a fit place to bring children up. I have taken great care to surround our lives with beautiful plants, flowers, pets and happiness. These are part of childhood and our home has great attraction for all children. We are always surrounded with them, even today, after all our sorrow and horror; life – that is life within the home – is almost back to normal.

FIVE

CURSE OF THE PAISNELS

Ted Paisnel and I were married quietly in St Helier on 1st July 1959. I felt very happy, for it was just over a year since I had lost my father and now here I had a man who, in many respects, even down to the little mannerisms, was very, very like him. All the omens seemed good and I felt that Ted's family welcomed my coming.

Although little more than what many people might consider an ordinary labourer, I knew that Ted had a deep creative instinct. He had already spoken to me about his desire to leave something behind in the world by which he could be remembered. Which would live after he had gone.

Little did we know or imagine what kind of memories he would leave behind him when he finally left the island or this life – he has indeed left us all with something by which he could be remembered.

He planted trees in many different parts of the valleys, and when he saw how we cooked certain herbs, he planted these wild all over the island. Almost as soon as we moved into Maison du Soleil, he was full of enthusiasm for rebuilding the house and landscaping the garden. The direct result of this was that, impressed by his enthusiasm and ideas, I suggested to him that he should cease hiring himself out as a labourer and stone-mason and set up on his own account as a builder and contractor. This, in due course, he did.

Yet I was soon to discover that Ted Paisnel bore many of the symptoms of a manic-depressive; heights of enthusiasm, one might even say euphoria, were matched by occasions of deepest apathy. He did eventually build more rooms in our part of Maison du Soleil, four bedrooms with hot and cold water in each, built-in cupboards and wardrobes, beautiful interior granite walls and indoor gardens. But it took him seven years strugling alone, and the effort of doing this was followed so often by mindless procrastination, when mentally I found myself unable to reach him. For example, he had us all scurrying around one day clearing everything out of one room, so that he could commence operations sharp at 8 o'clock the next morning.

'I'm going to put a new sink unit in there' he said and then went on to list other improvements he intended making. Come the next morning, a Sunday, he was still in his bed at 11 a.m. Then, when he did rise, the rest of the day was spent reading the Sunday newspapers. I found the whole thing infuriating, as all the water supplies had been turned off and I'd filled bowls and basins with water so that I could cook meals and make tea an so on. By 4 p.m., there was nothing for it but to shift all the stuff back in that we had spent the previous day so laboriously moving out. And so, another week went by and nothing was done. This, I might say, happened time and again. He would have sudden bouts of energy – 'I'm going to put some lintels in today,' or something like that; sometimes, he would, indeed, do as he promised; other times, his enthusiasm evaporated almost as suddenly as it was aroused. But great enthusiasm was always followed by sheer apathy. I cannot think of him as an intense person, but simply as basically lazy, lethargic and apathetic; a man who seemed to spend all his spare time reading, sleeping or watching T.V. This is not entirely a fair picture, for he had the capacity for extreme hard-work at certain times.

On one occasion – it was in March 1960 when I was sick and when one of the dreadful attacks took place (in fact it was when they all started in earnest) he made me a rockery. In between caring for me and the children with constant devotion he worked like a man possessed of unnatural strength to make this rockery of granite – not a small one but with cider press pieces and wheels which normally take four men and machines to move. He lifted them unaided with the use of a crowbar and finished the rockery in time to give me a lovely surprise. He included a toadstool of granite, and with the cement left over he made a huge (and quite ugly) toad with green marbles for eyes. Now the C.I.D. tell me that even that has black magic significance.

But he rarely made a sustained effort to finish anything. Whenever anything aroused his interest or enthusiasm, then he was capable of displaying splendid energy. Otherwise, he seemed to have his nose in some book or newspaper.

Within a few days of our marriage, Ted Paisnel disillusioned me rather sharply. Quite abruptly and violently, I saw a facet of

70

his personality very different from that which he had been at such great pains to display to me during our four months of courtship. The suave, slightly man-of-the-world figure, the man who had knocked about a bit but who was, nevertheless, kind and marvellous with the children up at the Home, turned suddenly into a rough, coarse, Jersey farm labourer. It was an extraordinary metamorphosis. Bad language suddenly flowed from him in a quite unnecessary way – it was bloody this and bloody that, swearing in French and English. I was really astounded. And he seemed so quick-tempered and quarrelsome. Inside the first month of our marriage, I had begun to see him in a very much different light to the mildly Prince Charming person I had previously known. He had several unholy rows with his parents – heaven knows what about, as they all spoke rapidly in Jersey-French. Complaints, particularly from English customers, which brought out his dislike of the English, made him angry. Over the years I became used to his violent tempers – he would suddenly flare up and sweep all the cups and saucers off the table or sweep all the objects on our sideboard on to the floor in a fit of temper. He would kick a chair or break the radio. Then, suddenly, his blind rage would evaporate and he used to be all right again.

Although shocked and considerably tensed by this unexpected change of personality, I was not prepared at first to make matters worse by standing up and telling him off at this early stage of our life together. After all, I already had one broken marriage behind me and I intended to tread very softly so far as this one was concerned. But our first major row could not be long delayed.

I owned two terrier bitches – I had been trying my hand as a dog-breeder before my marriage to Ted. They could be often noisy and would sometimes squabble and fight among themselves; but these sudden quarrels would be come and gone in a moment. Ted, of course, had been marvellous with them before we married, patting them on the head, playing with them and making me feel that here was a man who loved both children and dogs and seemed to have an extraordinary empathy with them – as I have indicated, one would have had to have the perspicacity of a Machievelli to fathom the man. This day, however, when the dogs began barking and squabbling, Ted went over and with an oath picked the two animals up and knocked their heads together in the most violent way imaginable.

As my children were both present along with some of the

71

foster children from the home – I think with every justification – I lost my temper and went for him in turn. We had a really serious row.

'I'm not going to allow this sort of thing!' I stormed at him. 'That was a dreadful thing to do – and especially in front of the children!'

'I don't give a damn!' he roared back, 'I'm the master of this house and nobody's going to dictate to me, not even you!' And he stormed out of the house.

I did not see him for another three days – he was obviously in a terrible huff. It is impossible to describe how upset I was and how I felt. I was as much astounded by his behaviour as, I suppose, anxious for the future of our marriage. Then he came back – I suppose he must have stayed in his parents' house in the meantime – and just carried on as though we had never had a cross word.

He also upset me by his manner towards his mother and sister, who lived next door to us, at the rear of the main house, with his sister's husband and two children. I thought his sister was a very friendly girl and both her children and her husband seemed very nice. To start with, we appeared to get on with each other marvellously and it did seem to me that it was going to be very pleasant to be part of such a friendly family. But when Ted walked in one day and found the two of us chatting together, he flew into a blind rage. When she had left, Ted wanted to know what we had been discussing.

'I don't want you to encourage her!' he insisted. 'I don't like the things she'll talk about to you – she'll only upset you.'

Ted said that he thought his mother and sister were inclined to gossip too much about the sexual side of peoples lives. I was never one to discuss our personal life or to listen to anything that was said about him or his past. I told him I had no intention of discussing our sex life with anyone – in fact I find that being told about that aspect of other peoples' lives can be extremely embarrassing and irritating.

I was constantly on edge when they talked in case they did speak about the subject, thinking that Ted might come in in the middle of the conversation. He was so aggressive that I had to use a great deal of skill in changing the subject and diverting the talk to more general topics. Eventually he seemed to discourage them altogether from coming to see us. Quarrels seemed to come from nowhere and we stopped visiting. I was unhappy about the constant bickering among the family, particularly as my own family had lived in such harmony at the children's home. Gradually I drifted back to more and more work at the home.

Certainly it was common knowledge that mother and daughter quarrelled seriously about Ted, but when families are under stress it is human to say cruel things to one another. In any case the island is known for its gossip and rumour – as are all small communities in the world. So it is wise not to take anything said about others too seriously, difficult though this is when it concerns one's own family. I never heard anything of significance said about Ted – nothing that would have connected him with the crimes of which he was later accused.

I have already said that the woman, with whom he lived during the war, found him a 'perfect lover', with nothing odd or kinky about his attitudes. For my own part, I have to say that one of the reasons why I never suspected that he was the beast who was terrorizing the island was because he seemed to me to have such a low sex-drive. It never occurred to me that anyone whom the newspapers could describe as 'a sex-fiend', who had assaulted and raped women and children, could be anything other than an enormously over-sexed person. I am a normal, warm-blooded woman and was only too anxious to respond to Ted's advances; and right from our wedding-day, we had decided to have children as soon as we could.

I can only say that our love-making proved less than satisfactory. It is very difficult to find an explanation for this unless one takes into account two things. The first is that possibly the normal love-making process, particularly within the matrimonial state, was becoming less and less attractive to him; that only abnormal forms, even at that stage, were capable of arousing him. The police have produced a graph showing how the purely sexual element – the really fierce sex-drive – seemed to be becoming less and less important in relation to his assaults, so that towards the end, shortly before his arrest, his attacks had become more and more of a technically-criminal nature, rather than cases of real rape.

I certainly thought he had a low sex-drive. But it seemed to me at the time – and even today I still feel the same way – that both his mental and physical approaches to me were also wrong. I have said that he considered me 'a goddess' (this was the word he used himself) and I think he set me on a pedestal. Since his arrest and sentence, he has written to me several times and in one

73

of his letters, he returns to this theme. 'When I married you, I reached for a star and a farmhorse like me could never keep up with a thoroughbred like you'.

His approach was mild and gentle, indeed quite timid; possibly too timid. And he had an extraordinary fetish about being clean. When I met him, he was always well-dressed, except when wearing his working clothes, but he was never a dandy. Once we were married, I encouraged him to use after-shave lotion and bought him a bottle, although I was careful not to *force* or nag him in any way to use it. I have mentioned his persecution complex – this was one of the main faults he said he found with his first wife; she used to nag him, he claimed, which is one reason why I tried to tread warily.

There was an extraordinary *musty* smell about him, which I really could not explain – although an explanation has now been advanced. I realize now that this should have struck an immediate chord in my mind because when the attacks were at their height, some of the women and children who were assaulted, described their assailant as having 'a musty or musky smell'. However, with hindsight, everything, naturally, becomes that much clearer but it was a detail which never made the impression on me that, perhaps, it should. It is only now, when he has been convicted and sentenced and when I sit down to remember all the details of our life together, that this kind of memory comes to the surface again, and I can see how naive I was not to put two-and-two together. I have since been told that the musty smell was some countryside substance that only Ted knew about that he rubbed over himself. This had the effect of stopping dogs in their tracks, making them docile, so he could enter premises at night.

Although, so far as I could detect, Ted washed and cleaned himself regularly, I did find that this peculiar musty sort of smell was still inclined to hang about him all the time. Certainly the bedroom which he occupied up until 1968 when he moved into his own quarters on the corner of Maison du Soleil, retains this awful musty smell to this day – exactly the same smell that so affronted Detectives Marsh and Lang when they broke into the secret room. I tried to get my son to move into this bedroom after Ted had moved out, but he refused to sleep there until I had got rid 'of that awful smell'. So I washed the carpet several times with Dettol; I burned incense and joss sticks, I tried a dozen different things to get rid of it, yet the smell still remains.

I cannot remember now whether I made some remark about

the smell to Ted or not. I recall that I said something about how strongly his hair smelled and gave this as my reason for encouraging him to use the after-shave lotion I bought him. Anyhow, this led to a rather extraordinary procedure on his part of washing himself in disinfectant. In a very short time, I couldn't bear the smell – I didn't quite know which was the worst, the musty smell or the other. I must say, too, that I believe that love-making should be a spontaneous thing. This kind of *clinical* approach certainly was discouraging to a woman.

Looking back now, it was a combination of all these factors – the dettol, the musty smell, the clinical approach to the matter of intercourse and Ted's rather tentative methods of love-making – with me at least – that made this aspect of our married life rapidly grow less than satisfactory. Whatever my initial feelings, of course, I was always ready to be aroused, but even when I managed to overcome my prejudices, Ted invariably failed. More often than not, to put it bluntly, he was simply impotent.

Nonetheless, I did conceive a baby. Six months later, however, I had a miscarriage. Ted's reactions were, to some extent, normal enough – he regretted deeply, as I did, the loss of our baby. Then, for the first time, however, he raised this matter of the so-called Curse of the Paisnels.

'It's the Curse,' he told me. 'There'll be no more males born in the Paisnel family.'

I pointed out that his relatives had successfully had children.

'I'm the end of my line,' he insisted. 'But it's a good thing. The Paisnels have always been wicked. Right through the centuries, they've been wicked and they should all be wiped out.' I particularly remember him saying that they had been 'rapists' and had been violent, throughout the centuries.

'Oh, the way you romance about things' I said. He was extremely proud of his French ancestry and particularly of the connection which he believed he had with the French noble family of Paynel, who had owned the castle and estates of Hambye in Normandy also large tracts of land in Jersey in the Middle Ages. 'Today is today,' I told him. 'And don't try and tell a woman who's just lost her baby that it's because she's cursed.'

In due course, I again conceived and was eventually delivered of a lovely little baby girl. To my sorrow, this poor child was born with rheumatoid arthritis, though it seems to be leaving her and she is improving every year now.

75

'There is goes again – the Curse!' insisted Ted, 'she was never meant to be normal.'

It might be argued that I should have paid more attention to all the things Ted said – and to have linked his curious ideas with the attacks on women and children. Again, this is hindsight, for it was not until his arrest and the discovery of the secret room that the question of black magic entered into the case at all. It ignores, too, the fact that I am a fairly practically-minded sort of person, with a rational approach to most matters. It is certainly true that I have consulted a faith-healer in connection with my daughter's deformity – but this was only after I had lost all hope in doctors. Possibly because I am a Londoner, I was inclined to dismiss most of the ideas held by the Paisnel family as island superstitions. I listened to them talk about curses and inexplicable cures which, I ought to realize now, I should have recognized as signs that they were, to put it mildly, 'susceptible' to witchcraft. But I paid almost no attention to this kind of talk and never took it seriously. Anymore than I took seriously Ted's ramblings about being descended from a noble French family or when he claimed the Paisnels had been 'violent' and 'rapists' throughout the ages. Even when he told me, 'there's a lot in black magic, you know – and people can be cursed by black magic' it seemed to me to be so much idle chatter. I remained totally sceptical; indeed, indifferent. If it made Ted happy, well, that was that. His trouble, I used to think, was that he read too much – 'you know me, Joan, I'll read anything' he used to say. I thought he had delusions of grandeur – it was slightly ridiculous, it seemed to me, listening to a man who was little better than a labourer prattling on about his noble ancestors. Even if I had believed all he said, however, why should I have connected any of this with the assaults? Many men have a Walter Mitty outlook on life – but that doesn't mean that they are monsters.

It was shortly after our daughter's birth that Ted and I stopped living together as man and wife. There was no sudden dramatic break between us; we just drifted apart. I, indeed, had the feeling, to some extent, that Ted was drawing away from me and my little family. Gradually he seemed to have less inclination to make love to me – which, at the time, I put down to two reasons; the first, that following my miscarriage and my daughter's unfortunate illness, he really was frightened of what might happen to any further children we might have and the second, that his attitude towards me was too respectful and, in a sense, to adoring. For my own part, I found it more and more difficult to have sexual relations with him in view of the bitter rows we had during the day; rows brought on by his quite irrational fits of temper. Soon, therefore, we decided to sleep in separate bedrooms.

One thing some people might find it difficult to understand is how, while we were both occupying the same part of Maison du Soleil and before Ted had built himself his offices and bed-sitting room at the top of the lane, I had no inkling of what he might have been up to. After all, I must have been aware of his movements?

To people living a suburban life, this idea is, perhaps, justi-fiable. Indeed, to people living regular lives of any kind – a 9 to 5 existence, if you like – it may be difficult to envisage the way we lived; or better, the way Ted lived. Ted Paisnel. from his child-hood, had led an easy-going, totally irregular way of life – although, I have no doubt, he had to toe the line while in England and Wales. He lived a completely free, independent sort of existence, coming and going at all hours just as he pleased. Although I was English, he was a Jerseyman, with all the habits, peculiarities and customs of a rural Jerseyman and so I never felt that it was up to me to interfere.

He would look out the door and then remark, 'It's a beautiful night, luv – I think I'll go for a walk.' Or he would say, 'I think I'll do some fishing tonight.' I was well aware that he had been living in this way since he had been a very young lad and as a mature person, anxious to make a go of her marriage, it never occurred to me to say, 'Oh, no, you mustn't go out' or, indeed, query his right to do so, in any way.

Nor is it such an unusual thing for a Jersey countryman to spend a night away from home fishing. If one goes down to St Catherine's pier any night there will be several men fishing there. Ted himself has often taken my son with him on these fishing expeditions. I have myself gone down to St Helier pier at one o'clock in the morning to pick up my son and have left Ted happily fishing away there. I cannot remember a night, either, when he said 'I think I'll go fishing,' that he did not bring fish back. In the morning, there would always be a catch lying on the lawn. Although he became a vegetarian himself, he did not consider eating fish a breach of vegetarianism. If I were asked to state categorically, 'Did Ted bring home fish every night he said he had been out fishing?' I'd have to answer truthfully that I could not be entirely sure; the impression I had *at the time* was that he did;

but I never kept a check. Although I know that he used several other methods to deceive me, I have no doubt that he genuinely loved fishing. I remember that after a good night's fishing, he always looked so happy and glowing with health.

An extraordinary aspect of his later attacks on children were that he carried them out under such extraordinary conditions; most of them took place when it was *pouring with rain*. Detective Marsh had described it as 'mind-boggling' that a man would take a child from its warm bed, lead it out into a nearby field with a rope round its neck and there assault it or commit a sodomy while it was *teeming with rain*. There has to be an explanation, of course, and it is this; once the police began to use tracker dogs in the case, Ted nearly always picked a showery or rainy night for his odious crime so that the dogs could not follow the scent.

I certainly got used to seeing him come home, wet and bed-raggled, with grass seeds and similar things clinging to him. Why wasn't I suspicious then? Well, I remember remarking once, 'My, you're in a state!' and he explained, 'What do you expect, I've been tickling trout up in Grands Vaux?' Perhaps I should explain that there are several reservoirs in what is called Water-works Valley and a lake in Grands Vaux and it was there, he gave me to understand, that he spent most of his nights fishing (it was also, incidentally, the area where many of the attacks took place). Once he had explained to me that 'tickling trout' involved lying down on the wet bankside and dipping his arm into the water so that he could get his hand under the bellies of the trout, it was natural for me to accept his bedraggled state.

On the whole, Ted and I remained fairly happy together (apart from certain alarums and excursions due to his temper) up until a short time after the birth of our daughter. He was at his best for a while after she had been born – very kind and con-siderate. I can recall him standing in the doorway and looking out at the night sky and saying, 'I think I'll take a walk, luv, but you needn't wait up – and I won't disturb you when I get back.' At this time, I was still breast-feeding the baby and had to waken at four-hourly intervals. 'I know you need your sleep,' he would add. We were still, of course, sharing the same bedroom.

Once or twice I came downstairs in the early hours to get some-thing for the baby and there was Ted, stretched out on the settee, a woolly cap on his head, fast asleep. I'd think, 'How thoughtful – lying there in that uncomfortable way, just because he doesn't want to disturb us!'

78

When you add this kind of behaviour to the willing work he continued to put in at the home, where the children still gathered round him shouting, 'Uncle Ted! Ted! Come and play with us,' and I watched the way he handled them, wiping noses, soothing small hurts, putting the younger ones on their potties, flinging them in the air and catching them – behaving, indeed, as though he were their natural uncle, it was impossible for me to conceive that there might be any real evil in him. An exhibition of bad temper is one thing; evil is quite another. To me, in a way, also, a violent temper such as Ted's had a strong *masculine* quality to it; such a quality, indeed, that it must have subconsciously reinforced my inability to see him as a homosexual.

Nor do I see how I could have spotted anything sinister about his absences from the house for several reasons – apart from the fact that even before he had taken up his abode in his own bed-sitter, he came and went much as he pleased. Many evenings he went out saying he was going next door to play cards with his sister and her husband; it never occurred to me to check this story and only since his arrest have I discovered that he was lying. Then there was his fishing. Or his walking. And of course, he continued these habits even during periods when there were no attacks – had he restricted these night excursion to periods only when attacks were taking place, then my suspicions *might* have been aroused. But I saw his rambles as a way of life with with him; something that he had been doing since he was a boy. There was nothing *abnormal* about him going out the way he did.

He also did a lot of work at night, on his own behalf. It took him over seven years to build the additional rooms and gardens he added to our part of Maison du Soleil, apart from his own bed-sitter and offices, and he did it all for less than £1,000.

He put the whole lot together in a quite amazing way on a veritable shoestring, gathering bits and pieces wherever he could find them. Behind our walls, for instance, instead of using steel rods to reinforce the stone and cement, he used old iron bedsprings. He did the most astonishing things in order to save money – for I ought to emphasize that from the first day I married him until the day he was arrested. Ted Paisnel never had any money; indeed, we lived with an overdraft almost constantly at £1,000.

I can give one or two examples. I remember one day, one of his workmen remarking, 'Listen, Ted, they're pulling down a

79

hotel and there's a couple of marvellous staircases there that they're going to burn. But you'll have to go and get them yourself – I can't help you.' Ted went to have a look and I remember him telling me one teatime, 'Those staircases are worth at least £40 each.'

'Why can't you go down and offer the man a price, then?'

'Because they won't let me have them, that's why.' A look of bitterness crossed his face. 'And all they're going to do with them is put them on a bonfire – we saw it as we were passing in the van.'

The next morning, to my astonishment, in some mysterious way two excellent staircases had made their appearance at the back of the house where Ted usually keeps his supplies of building materials.

'How did they get there?' I asked him.

He told me that he had gone out in the middle of the night, dragged each of the staircases off the bonfire and had then made two journeys, each time hoisting a part of the staircase on to his shoulders and dragging the whole lot, *not* by road, which would have been extraordinary enough, but across the fields, across ditches and through hedges, for a couple of miles! He did not want anybody to catch him dragging the staircases along the road, so he had carried and pulled them across the fields. I found it incredible that one man could find the strength to haul one of those things even a short distance; but to haul *two*, and both across the *fields* seemed to me a really extraordinary feat of strength. If it had not been for the evidence out in the yard, frankly I would never have believed him.

On another occasion, I remember him saying, 'There's a house being pulled down in Rozel (one of the coastal areas of St Martin parish). There's a sink there that would do just nice for our girl's bedroom. And what do you think they're going to do with it – dump it. That's the trouble with the rich, they just throw things away.'

I believe that that was one of the nights he came home very late and I found him lying asleep on the settee; it was probably around three or four in the morning. When I went down to the lounge, my movements must have wakened him.

'You got in late then?' I asked for he had not come up to the bedroom, fulfilling his promise not to waken me and the baby.

'Oh, yes,' he said in an off-handed way, 'but I got it! And then by the time I walked there, my feet hurt so much that I sat down on the shore and put them in the sea.'

Nothing, really, could have been more natural. It really would have demanded extraordinary insight to connect him, on the strength of this kind of thing, with the horror then going on in the island.

I have mentioned his resentment of the rich – which, when you look at it, seems an extraordinary contradiction in view of his obsession with his 'aristocratic ancestors'. But Ted always insisted that he had Communist leanings and in his usual oblique way, gave me to understand that he had once been a Communist and a member of the party. Certainly he used to inveigh against middle-class people with a display of indignation often amounting to a real rage. I remember up at the Home on one occasion he burst out, 'There's so much waste among the middle class. Look at little Georgie there riding around on that rusty bike and I've been to a place recently where they'd bought the most beautiful bikes for their children – and they are just left there rusting in the garden. They buy their kids anything they want – and then the kids don't take a speck of notice! These families with money! Do you know what I'm going to do?'

'No, what?'

'One of these nights, I'm going to go and get one of these bikes – and give it to little Georgie here.'

He must have forgotten about his promise for, anyway, little Georgie never got his bike – not that I would have permitted him to accept it.

His resentment against the better-off was no act, however; whatever the truth about his 'Communist' ideas, he unquestionably hated those who appeared to have more money than they needed. One of the strange facts about his attacks was that they were invariably on children of well-to-do parents – almost as though he were taking some dark, curious revenge of his own.

He certainly appeared to have a kind, almost philantrophic streak in him. Was it genuine or was it part of the image he consciously set out to create? I'm afraid I am not competent to answer this – it is quite impossible to tell where the real Ted Paisnel leaves off and the false one takes over; or whether, indeed, there were not several Ted Paisnels, all of them, at various times, utterly genuine.

There is no question in my mind, from all that I have learned since I got to know him, that he genuinely did try to help people

81

during the German Occupation. On one occasion, I'm told, he stole an animal from the Germans – probably a pig – and kept it hidden in a shed until it was ready for slaughtering; then he distributed the food among needy people. I have spoken about the good work he did at the children's home – he lavished an extraordinary amount of time (and in his case, time was also money) repairing windows and roofs and doing all sorts of painting jobs. Shortly after we were married, we heard of a local woman whose husband had run off leaving her with seven children to bring up. Ted piled in with tremendous enthusiasm to get a big parcel of clothes together for the family and I was with him when he drove down to the woman's house and delivered it. He was still doing the same kind of thing up to three weeks before his arrest.

When he had eventually got his own business going, I remember on once occasion when I was doing the accounts for him, I queried an unpaid bill. 'What about this one – you put a new window in ?'

He came across and looked. 'Oh, *her !* She's an old lady – I'm not charging her anything.'

As part of the children's home scheme, I had obtained a licence to keep three foster children at Boulivot (at Maison du Soleil), as overflow. Ted was always especially kind to these unfortunate children and the harder their circumstances, the kinder he was to them; in other words, anything for the under-dog. Sometimes, the parents of these children were rather slow in paying the fee for their upkeep – which meant that the children were, in effect, being housed and fed at Ted's expense. I felt it my duty under such circumstances to tell him.

'We'll keep 'em, anyway' I remember Ted saying once, 'the parents probably are worried about something else and haven't the money'. On one occasion, one of the parents was £70 in arrear – I pointed out to Ted that I really ought to report him to the authorities who might force him to pay.

'Oh don't worry the poor fellow' said Ted, 'he's probably trying to support three or four other kids. If the worst comes to the worst, couldn't we *adopt* the kid properly ?'

I am positive that none of this was a pose. He genuinely had good and generous impulses; he genuinely did try to help the unfortunate; he genuinely did feel a sense of resentment against those who had too much when he could see that others were in dire want.

82

So far as money was concerned, he was never mean or tight-fisted. As I say, he was always in debt, although Maison du Soleil and the farm that goes with it, of which he could have expected to inherit a major part at least, is today worth a small fortune. I know, however, that he worried about his overdraft. He would come up the lane from his own office sometimes and open the door, his face creased with worry. 'The overdraft's over the limit, I'm afraid – what's the situation? Have you enough fosterage money coming in to take care of the children all right?'

'Yes, I have,' I'd reply.

'Well, could you maybe keep some the bills you owe back for a few days then?'

No tantrums; no display of rage of anxiety – just a good-natured request to help and a kind inquiry to make sure that the children would not suffer.

Looking back over my years as Ted Paisnel's wife – and in the light of what I now know – I can see that the extraordinary oscillations of behaviour on his part were sure signs of a schizo-phrenic condition. All that seems quite clear now – and possibly had I been trained as a psychiatrist. I might have tumbled to the fact that he badly needed medical treatment. I might have tumbled to the fact that he was the Jersey sex-fiend. When one lives day by day with someone, however, their behaviour becomes something that you tend to take for granted. You become inured to the outbursts of violent temper just as you become grateful for the tender gestures.

I had, as I have already said, plenty of examples of his vicious temper. As the years went on, I became used to these storms – used to them in the sense that I did not find them unexpected; they still did have the power to upset me terribly. You cannot watch a man sweep everything standing on a sideboard on to the floor with a vicious swipe of his arm without feeling a tremor run through you. Often the slightest thing seemed to upset him. He would come storming into the lounge or kitchen shouting that one of the kids had left something lying in the drive – an un-reasonable display of rage quite out of keeping with the enormity of the alleged crime. One, in a sense, had to be prepared for irrational outbreaks at any time and for the most trivial of reasons. Certainly, it was hardly the most comfortable way to live and on two occasions I moved out of Maison du Soleil and went to stay with my mother at the home, my mind made up to obtain a divorce. On each occasion, however, I was persuaded to a reconciliation and returned to the house, although Ted and I never slept together again. For a while he would strive to keep his temper under control. Then I would hear violent language in the lane and wait, often trembling a little, for the full wrath to descend on me. Sometimes he would come storming in, kicking up a fuss about some little thing; other times the language might be directed at his workmen or even some harmless object; sometimes he would stop before he reached me, his anger spent and I'd watch him stagger back up in the lane, his head bowed, his whole figure crouched with worry and anxiety and then he would stop and stare at something and scratch his head, as though puzzled. I remember watching him do this on one occasion and thinking to myself, 'Poor devil, something's got him all worried. And the way he keeps us and works so hard on our behalf.'

I recalled how good he was to his step-children. Only one child was his, after all; but he treated all of them equally. He bought a beautiful illustrated encyclopaedia for all the children; he paid for piano lessons and ballet lessons for them and helped send one to secretarial school; he helped my son buy an electric guitar plus an amplifier and when Ted's sister complained about the noise, built a hut in the middle of the field, well away from the house, where, it was hoped, he could make as much noise as he liked without disturbing anyone (alas, his sister still complained).

He might grumble a bit, as most men do, when asked to do something at an awkward moment. While we were still sharing the same bedroom, I recall, the children came to us – about midnight I think – to explain that one of their guinea pigs had got loose and Lord only knows why they couldn't have told me earlier. We were both in bed, but not yet asleep.

'One of the guinea pigs is loose,' I remember telling Ted.

All I got was a mumble from the depths of a pillow.

'It's lost,' I repeated, 'and a dog might get it while it's wandering about.'

'What do you want me to do?' grumbled Ted his voice a mixture of resignation and exasperation.

'Well, we can't let in wander about all night, can we?'

'Oh, bloody hell, then!' he said, sitting up and throwing back the bedclothes. 'It's a nice state of affairs that I've got to go out and search for a missing guinea pig at this time of the night!' Still grumbling, he put on his dressing gown and I got up, too; and then, both of us still in our dressing gowns, we went out into the garden and began looking around. Ted, of course, had an uncanny knack where animals were concerned and it would take him only a comparatively short time to find it. I recall him handing me the guinea pig and smiling.

'Now are you satisfied?'

'Oh, Ted! It's for the children, after all.'

And, for a moment, our relationship was very warm and human.

The year before his arrest, one of my little canaries got loose. I noticed it was missing and even though it was dark, I went out searching for it. I carried a torch and eventually I discovered it, perched on the troughing of his sister's house next door. Every now and then I shone the torch up at it, hoping to drive it down – all the time aware that any any moment, his irate sister might stick her head out the window and demand to know what I was doing; it was, after all, gone past midnight.

I was standing there, in the dark, trying to work out how to get the canary down, when Ted happened along.

'What's the matter, luv?'

'It's the canary' I replied. Then I pointed the torch to where the little creature was sitting perched, apparently quite asleep.

'Why didn't you call me?'

'Oh, I didn't want to bother you.'

'Hold on.'

He went away and came back in a moment with a long ladder. He put this up against the wall, right beside his sister's window and just below where the canary sat. Then he went up the ladder as silent and stealthily as a shadow and plucking the canary off the troughing, brought it down and handed it to me.

'Now, get to bed.'

Looking back now, I realize that this alone ought to have alerted me to Ted's potential ability to be the Jersey sex-fiend; normally his sister is an alert woman who hears the slightest thing that goes on around her. If I, for example, had tried to put a heavy ladder against her wall like that and had tried to scale it, she would undoubtedly have heard the bumping and scraping and the sounds of me climbing up. Ted did it all so silently that he made no more noise than a ghost. No wonder he could enter houses without anyone hearing him.

He knew everything about nature, of course; under other circumstances, he might have become a famous naturalist. When we first got married, he used to intrigue me, the way he could pick birds out of a tree in the dark. I remember one evening going out to post a letter and he walked along with me. Suddenly, he stopped and putting his finger to his mouth, said 'Shush'. Then he tiptoed very gently over to a hedge and again whispered, 'Watch this'. I saw him reach into the hedge – I couldn't actually make out anything there – and take out a sleeping sparrow in his hand. He held it there for a moment for me to look at it, then, ever so gently reached his hand back into the hedge, putting the bird back where he had found it – and without once wakening it.

He used to fascinate the children every bit as much as he did me. One night, just when I had got my small daughter ready for bed, he came into the sitting room and said, 'Come quickly, I've got something to show you.' As the child ran towards him, I protested, 'What do you mean, taking the child out at this hour of the night?'

'Oh, I must take her' he insisted, his face full of enthusiasm, 'there's nest of hedgehogs down the field – and they're all babies.'

'How on earth do you know that?' I demanded.

'Oh, I've been walking round the field' he explained.

It was like this all the time. We would all be out walking when suddenly he would find a vole or other rare field animal. I could be walking the fields of Jersey for years by myself and never sight a vole. With Ted around, you seemed to *feel* the little creatures all about you; you became aware of that other world, the world of birds and animals, that, certainly, a townswoman like myself was normally never aware of. Only a few months before his arrest, he shouted to me one beautiful night, 'Come here, Joan, come quickly – did you ever hear this before?'

I left the lounge and joined him outside in the back garden. It was a still, moonlight night, with the whole countryside bathed in soft light.

'Listen!' he said.

I listened. But all I could hear was the marvellous stillness.

'I can't hear anything' I said, after a moment or two.

'Go on, listen!' he insisted.

Again I tried to listen. But even after a minute or so, I could still hear nothing.

'Migrating birds' he whispered. 'Now listen to their whistle – the whistle of their wings'. And, do you know, after straining for another moment or so, I could actually hear them! I was astonished; and they were so high!

'They must be a mile high,' breathed Ted. 'And yet you can hear them.' His whole body was tensed with suppressed excite-

86

ment. I can only record that it was one of the most marvellous experiences of my life.

On Sundays, he would often take us out into one of the valleys and it was a revelation. He would park the car seemingly at random, then get out, walk into a field or over to a hedge and call, 'Look here, kids' – and when they went across, there would be the nest of a moorhen or some other rare bird. He seemed to know the habits and habitats of every bird and animal on the island.

To me, he remains a complete enigma. I think of the man bringing home a big catch of fish in a bucket and remarking kindly, 'I know you don't eat fish – but give them to some of your friends'. I remember the man who fixed the slates and windows at the home, whistling pleasantly to himself, stopping only to shout a cheery remark to one of the youngsters. I remember all the work he did at the Home curing dry rot there; he took the tower off the building and found it full of dry rot.

'Look at this' he said, showing me the rotten beams. 'If I hadn't taken this off, the whole thing would have fallen through the roof one of these days and right into the bathroom while one of the kids was there'.

And then he went and persuaded some of the Jersey merchants to provide new beams and girders free, insisting that it was a noble act of charity!

Even now, I still feel that he was not deceiving me but being genuinely thoughtful. Several times when I drew attention to work he had scheduled to do, he brushed it aside with the remark, 'I'll leave that little job until later – they're in no hurry. There's an old woman over in the valley who wants me to dig her garden; I'd better go and do it for her now the weather's right'. Later I learned that the woman with whom he had lived during the war and who had gone away from Jersey for a while, had returned and was living over in the Grands Vaux – did he go to dig the old lady's garden or did he go to see his old flame? I cannot be certain.

Ted was a good craftsman. I think most people will give him credit for that. When he tackled a job, he did it very well. He was so proud, indeed, of his work, that he used to leave his mark – the sign of a fish. I remember he built a new concrete post up at the home and he showed me the fish. 'Anywhere you see that sign in Jersey, you'll know I did the work,' he told me. What I didn't know was that he had reason for associating this sign with the great hero of his life, Gilles de Rais, the Black Baron. However, we shall deal with his obsession with this terrible man presently.

Yet if Ted were a good craftsman, I cannot say that he was a good businessman. He had two main failings – he was totally incapable of estimating a job properly, so that he constantly undertook work that was bound to cause him a loss. Again, and possibly more importantly, he was far too spasmodic a worker and too unreliable. Customers could never be certain if Ted was going to turn up or not.

He was a man of so many different moods and so many complex attitudes that I have the impression that he often deliberately did not turn up at a job just to spite his customers. That is, if they were English. He undoubtedly had an inferiority complex. A manifestation of this, I believe, was his obsession with his 'aristocratic ancestors'. Another was his curious snobbery; I once tried to get him to go on a builder's course of instruction to improve his craftsmanship and he rebuked me indignantly with the words, 'I've no intention of mixing with those peasants!' Another facet of this complex was his hatred of the English – he did not like the English; I think he thought English people were too arrogant. When he did not turn up for some customer, I invariably had to bear the brunt of their complaints, for Ted was off somewhere when they telephoned. At first I tried to put their complaints over to him, raising the subject in a mild and gentle way so as not to annoy him. But however tactfully I tried to put it, Ted would invariably explode.

'Every time I come home, you have some bloody tale about some bloody customer! You bloody English – you're always complaining!'

In the end, I got so fed up with this kind of verbal lashing, that I have up speaking to him and simply wrote him a note and pushed it under the door of his office. As sure as day follows night, I always got an explosive call on the inter-com, full of attacks on the English. 'Why don't they go back to their own island and leave this island alone!' he used to yell.

His predictable bouts of violent temper were something, I suppose, that I just got used to living with. I recall occasions over the years when I would be dressing the children, getting them ready for school when, through a window, I would catch a glimpse of him tearing down the lane on his way towards us and

I'd wonder, 'What in heaven's have we done now?' At first I answered him back when he stormed in, 'How dare you come in here and upset me and the children like this, just when they're getting read to go to school?' That, as I have already related, was the signal for him to sweep everything on to the floor or smash or kick something or fling cups and saucers across the room against the wall. By dinner time that evening, he was quiet as a lamb again. He would turn up and either ignore the storm of the morning or make light of it. Sometimes, as a peace offering, he brought a present for the children or perhaps a new plant for me. When I told him that he had upset the children so much that I couldn't send them to school, he would simply shrug. I think that despite his seeming love for children and all the work he did about the house, he really did not like domestic life and that the cares and worries of being father and husband were often too much for him.

I knew we really couldn't go on living together properly as man and wife as early as 1960 – shortly after I'd had my second miscarriage and I'd had to once again listen to Ted's doom-laden words about the Curse of the Paisnels. I tried to prepare the way by, in a semi-joking manner, remarking that many married people were still able to lead happy lives, even though they shared separate bedrooms. At this stage, I was steeling myself to make the break. I don't think, though, that the question of divorce ever really came into either of our minds – we both had broken marriages behind us and neither of us could quite see the advantage in destroying the lives of the children. In the end, we were to remain friends, but lead separate lives. He certainly made a better friend than husband.

The crunch, I suppose, came when I took our daughter, still only a baby, to England to have her disability diagnosed and to see if anything could be done for her. She spent eight weeks in hospital; then the doctors broke the news to me that her problem was incurable and that she would have to spend the rest of her life with a deformed hand. They warned me that I must guard against a worsening of her situation – I must try to give her a happy, contented home life and guard against too much emotional distress or upset of any kind.

I returned to Boulivot to find that Ted had behaved in an oddly callous way with my little clutch of chickens. He had kept them locked up in their henhouse for the whole eight weeks I had been away. My first act was to let them out. I made no attempt to remonstrate with Ted, however; the last thing I wanted in view of the doctor's advice, was a scene. He had been so delighted to see us return.

I was standing at the Aga cooker in the kitchen, preparing a meal, only two days after our return when suddenly a granite stone whizzed past my ear, and struck the wall. It was followed by another, then another and I turned to see Ted pelting me with those stones that one of the children had picked up off the beach. He kept flinging them at me, at the same time yelling, 'Will you keep your bloody chickens locked up – I've just planted some seeds down there!' One pebble, easily the size of a half-brick, might have killed me had I not seen it coming and ducked. The worst feature of all this, from my point of view, was that our daughter witnessed the whole thing. When Ted had calmed down – he always calmed down, even if he never apologized – I wrote him a long letter telling him we must arrange our lives so that whatever differences we had, our daughter would never again be upset by such scenes. It was the final break and from then on Ted occupied his own bedroom and later his own bed-sitter and never again showed violence. I never entered his private quarters, when he built the bed-sitter although he often invited me. We had an intercommunication system installed so that we could speak to each other without the need to leave our own accommodation. At first he even prepared his own meals, but later I persuaded him for his own sake to take his meals with the family.

On occasions, I walked down the lane with a letter or message for him and I remember now that when he opened the door to me, he rarely opened it very wide. What his reasons for this were, I cannot guess, unless he had one of his mistresses there at the time and did not want me to see her.

On the other hand, although we slept in different parts of the house we continued to live, in nearly all other respects, like an ordinary family. There was never a point when Ted, either by tacit agreement or otherwise, was barred from my part of the house. He continued to come in and out in the ordinary way, sitting down to read or watch T.V. or just talk. As a real marriage, however, ours had ceased to exist.

Until 1968, we occupied separate bedrooms in the same part of the house. Even before this, I had got used to Ted's irregular comings and goings, which included sleeping wherever the fancy took him or circumstances dictated. Some nights, I know, for

90

example, he slept on the settee in his parents' home. Even before he moved into his own bedsitter permanently he would sometimes go down there and sleep in his loft or workshop rather than disturb me and the children.

It was while he was still sleeping in the same part of the house however, that I experienced one of his most violent outbursts. Ted never carried a key to the house and normally I left the doors unlocked so that he could get in. As he was working hard at this period, doing a lot of overtime, he would generally not be home until about 11 p.m. – by which time the children and I were in bed. One week, however, he began stopping out later than ever, frequently not coming in until three or four in the morning. Before going out each morning, he put on a good suit and as I heard he was receiving telephone calls and letters from a certain girl at this time, I naturally assumed he had gone to meet her.

It was a week when the attacks had started again and I warned him that he had better take a key this time because I was not going to leave the doors unlocked with a maniac on the rampage again. He said nothing and I presumed he had taken one of the keys and locked the doors and went to bed.

It was have been at least 3 o'clock when I was awakened by this terrible shouting and hammering down below. I got up and went to the window and there was Ted below yelling, 'Open the bloody door, I'm not going to be shut out of my own place!'

I told him I had warned him to take a key.

'Never mind that! Open the bloody door.'

I told him I had no intention of opening the door if he was in a temper. Although I had learned it was best to try and placate him when he was in one of his moods, I had also found out that if he were thwarted, he might go away and his rage subside as suddenly as it had come.

When I refused to go down this time, however, his mood got even more ugly and he began to hammer and smash at the glass at the rear of the house. This is safety glass and however hard he hammered it, he could do no more than splinter it. Foiled, he went away and got some object (I could not see what it was in the dark) and threw it through the toilet window, and climbed through. Then he went up to his own bedroom and shut the door, without a further word to me. The next morning, I was unable to let the children use the toilet because there was glass all over the place. Yet when Ted got up, he painstakingly started mending the windows without even a word of complaint to me.

91

Why did I not go down and let him in? The answer is that I grew more and more frightened the more frantic his behaviour became. I had not gone down and let him in immediately because I thought he might go away and not disturb the children.

I have no way of knowing whether he had attacked anyone that night because not all the attacks were reported immediately and even when one learned later that there had been one, I never thought to associate Ted's behaviour or movements on these occasions with any of those attacks; one would have had to have been suspicious and keeping a constant check on him. To me, that terrible night was just another of Ted's outbursts – a display of bad temper with which I had become all too familiar.

SIX

TERROR BY NIGHT

Sometime about midnight on the night of Saturday/Sunday, 26th/27th March 1960, a 43-year-old woman, living in a fairly isolated cottage in the parish of St Martin, was awakened by the ringing of her telephone. She had been reading and had just dozed off when the telephone rang.

She got up and went downstairs, wondering who on earth could be calling her at that hour. When she lifted the receiver, there was a click and all she heard was the dialling tone. Imagining that it must be someone who had got a wrong number, she went back to bed and turning out the light, fell asleep again.

Sometime between 1 and 1.30 a.m., she believes, she was again awakened when her black labrador came up the stairs. It was not barking but making 'a very unusual noise' and she thought it might be ill – perhaps there was something wrong with the stove in the kitchen. She ordered it back down the stairs, but it refused to go. Feeling a little anxious because her husband was in hospital and the cottage was fairly isolated with fields behind and on either side of it and a lane in front – a cottage that could be easily observed from an old shed facing or from the surrounding hedges – she got up again and donning her dressing gown, spectacles and slippers, decided to go downstairs. At that moment, she 'heard a bump' and going to a window, opened it and looked out but could see nothing. With some trepidation, she decided to investigate.

She had almost reached the bottom of the stairs when abruptly the lights went out. At the same time she heard someone moving about in the living room. Desperately, she made a break for the telephone to call '999' but found the instrument dead. As she stood there in the dark, almost frightened out of her wits, the figure of a man appeared – she was able to make out his faint shadow 'because he carried a light torch'. She also noticed that he had 'a cloth or handkerchief' over his face. Almost at once he grabbed hold of her and said, 'I want some money – give me some money.'

'I haven't any money,' said the woman. He became very angry at this and in desperation the woman tried to think of anything valuable in the house. I've some jewellery but no money' she said. Then she suddenly remembered her purse. He allowed her to get it but when she offered it to him and he discovered it had only a few coppers in it, 'he threw it down with disgust'.

She then noticed that the kitchen door was open and almost as a way of distracting his attention, she said, 'Oh, the door's open. Did I leave it open?'

'Yes,' he said.

At something of a loss as to what to do next, the woman said, 'I haven't got any money – why don't you go?'

All this time she had hardly allowed her voice to rise above a whisper because her 14-year-old daughter was asleep in the room above and on no account did she want to waken her or let the man know she was there.

'No, I won't go – I want some money,' he said.

He then roughly ordered her to sit down and when she hesitated, he grabbed hold of her and pushed her down on to a chair. 'I've killed before – and I'll kill again!' he told her. She tried to struggle with him, but he forced her hands behind her back and tied them together.

'I tried to think what I could do. I tried to pull my wrists apart so that it would be easier to get away. He started to gag me and I heard my daughter getting up, so I tossed my head about and got the gag out of my mouth. I shouted to my daughter to stay where she was and to lock the door. But she came out because she knew something was wrong.' The man sprang up and began walking towards the stairs even as she heard her daughter on the landing.

Although her glasses had been knocked off in the struggle, the woman at once made a bolt for the open kitchen door and ran towards a farmhouse opposite. As she ran, the bonds holding her wrists loosened. There were two houses on the farm opposite but although in a frenzy she 'banged and knocked on the door, I couldn't make anybody hear and I could not see because my glasses had been knocked off and I am very shortsighted.' She broke a window, 'but still nobody heard me, so I ran back to the cottage.' When she got back there, there was no sign of either the man or her daughter. So once again she ran back to the farm 'and

94

this time somebody was up and he ran to the cottage and I rang the police.'

Back once more in the cottage, she could still see no sign of her daughter, so, despite her terror and being almost half-blinded without her glasses, the woman began running down the lane opposite the house calling to her daughter. There were several other lanes down which she might have been taken so 'it was useless'. After a long and fruitless search, she eventually went back to her cottage where she found her daughter. By this time there was also a policeman there. The girl's eyes were swollen, there were marks round her neck and she was bleeding from the nose. Her daughter ran to her and said, 'I've been raped – but thank goodness you're alive, mother.' All the woman could gasp out was, 'I thought you were dead!'

The girl's story was a terrible one. To the police who later saw her, it seemed clear that she had been brought near to the edge of death, for her eyes had 'popped' – which accounted for the swelling round them. When she heard the noise from the kitchen below and had gone out on to the landing the man had come up the stairs, grabbed her and put a rope around her neck. He tightened this to such a degree that she began to choke and she believed she had then passed out for a few moments (the police view was that the man had, in a symbolic sense, 'killed' the girl, but then brought her back to life – and medical opinion supported the theory than an extra twist would have been suffi-cient to kill her).

With the rope or cord still very tight round her neck, the girl was led from the house. She tried to struggle, but this only resulted in him tightening the noose even further. He led her across some fields, then down a bank and into a lane. As they were walking, he kept saying 'Jesus', or 'bejabbers,' and re-marks such as, 'Your mother is a stupid woman'. His accent seemed to her to be either Irish or French – certainly not pure Jersey.

She was taken up another bank and into a field, which she later identified as The Field of the Devil. Here the man told her he was going to rape her. He kept on saying 'your mother is a stupid woman' and added – the police think as part of his plan to plant misleading clues – 'I think my mother died of drink'. At one stage, with the noose tight around her neck, he told her, 'I'm going to kill you now,' and she said, 'Well, you'd better get on with it, then, hadn't you?'

He seemed nervous, had a quite voice and was rather hesitant. She thought her mother might be dead, but the man then kept telling her that he was 'going to take her to her mother'. Suddenly, he put a blindfold over her eyes and threw her to the ground, and then raped her. Afterwards, he suddenly got up and walked away. She got up, picked up the piece of rope that had been around her neck and ran home.

She was able to identify her assailant as slightly built, dark, with a cap and a thick, rough coat. He appeared to have a rather long forehead and his face had been covered with a dark mask. As to height, she came up to about his shoulder. Her mother identified the man as wearing a flat cap with a cloth round the lower part of his face. His coat was rough and baggy, similar to a duffle coat. He was not a young man, she thought, but probably between 30 and 40 and about 5 feet 7 inches in height.

Detective Chief Superintendent Ted Cockerham who investigated the case following the call to the police, discovered that the man had first entered a garden shed at the rear of the house and had taken an old pair of underpants, a spade and a garden dibber. He had used the underpants to gag the attacked girl's mother and the spade was left in the kitchen. The dibber had been found stuck in the ground at the rear of the house. The intruder had gained entry by breaking a large pane of glass in the kitchen window. A tray of fruit had been taken from the windowsill and put on the ground outside – some of the fruit had been eaten. The telephone wire had been *wrenched* out, not cut. A bottle of whisky had been removed from its position beside the master light-switch for the house – the switch itself had been turned off. A box of raw chicken was found lying on the floor of the kitchen – Cockerham decided it had been put there for the dog to east as a means of distracting it.

Dr David Scott-Warren who arrived at the house at 2.50 a.m., found that the woman had swollen lips, cuts and bruises while her daughter had multiple abrasions to legs and hands, nettle rash on the left thigh, abrasions on the neck and sub-conjunctival haemorrhages to both eyes. There was blood and mud on her pyjamas and although she was in a state of shock when he examined her, she was coherent. Significantly, there appeared to have been no penetration of the vagina.

Whoever the maniac was – and eventually my husband Ted Paisnel was found guilty of the attacks I have described above – the assaults on children continued. There was a pattern about them all, particularly the fact that the attacker usually struck on a Saturday (certainly always at week-ends) and that he was invariably described as 'wearing a mask.' On April 24th, 1960, a 14-year-old girl living at La Rocque awoke in the middle of the night to find a man – he had climbed in through a fanlight – standing over her bed. She screamed and taking fright, the man made off in a panic. The child could only say that her would-be assailant had been 'wearing a mask'.

On the evening of Saturday, 30th July 1960, an eight-year-old boy was watching T.V. at his home in La Blinerie when a man crawled in through a fanlight window, led him outside, indecently assaulted him and then led him back to his house and left him standing on his doorstep. The only description the child could offer was that his assailant had been wearing a 'khaki-coloured raincoat.'

For the rest of the year, the maniac – or maniacs – lay dormant. Then the attacks started up again. On Saturday, 18th February 1961, at Mont Cochon, a man entered a 12-year-old boy's bedroom and put a rope round his neck. The boy was led out of the house and into the garden of a house opposite but the would-be attacker appeared to have second thoughts for the boy was left there unharmed. The lad described the man as aged about 40 and 5 feet 6 inches tall. Three weeks later, on 4th March 1961, an 11-year-old boy living in St Saviour parish was awakened by an intruder who had apparently once again gained egress by the fanlight. This time the man tied the boys' own school belt round his neck, but even as he did so, the boy tumbled out of bed, falling to the floor with a resounding bump. This aroused the lad's father and the man, described as wearing a cap, and a raincoat and with 'a soft accent', leaped out of the window and made off. The man – if it were the same man – proved more successful on his next outing, which followed at approximately 1 a.m. on Sunday, 23rd April, in the parish of St Martin. An 11-year-old girl, sleeping in a lonely bungalow in St Martin parish, was roused by a man wearing a nylon stocking mask who whispered, 'Be quiet – or I'll kill your mother and father'. The child was too terrified to do anything but obey, although her parents were asleep in the next room. The man ordered her to put on her shoes, then blindfolded her with another nylon stocking and carried the terrified child, still in her nightclothes, to a muddy potato field where he brutally assaulted her. Following the attack, he coolly carried her back to the house.

Later, police found three well-used nylon stockings in the field, none of which, according to subsequent investigation, was owned by any woman living in the neighbourhood.

By this time, the terror has reached such proportions on Jersey, particularly among people living in isolated areas in the eastern half of the island, where all the attacks appeared to be concentrated, that the authorities decided to call on the assistance of Scotland Yard. Shortly before the last attack, 52-year-old Det/Superintendent Jack Mannings arrived in the island amid a calculated blaze of publicity. Welsh-born Mannings, known for his dapper taste in clothes, had gained a reputation for his penetrating methods and particular his persuasive interrogation of murder suspects. He had served in several notable positions in the Metropolitan Police – from busting some of the Soho crime gangs to inquiring into the causes of the Notting Hill race riots and even recovering jewellery stolen from Princess Alexandra in 1958. He had been a member of the Yard's Murder Squad, both as sergeant and superintendent and had received more than 20 commendations from the Commissioner of Police.

As parents adopted their own methods to combat the maniac – securely locking all doors and windows; buying a dog if they had not already got one; sleeping with coshes or pokers beside their beds – news was leaked to the press that Mannings' main worry was to prevent the maniac going too far the next time and giving the rope he put round his victims an extra twist that would lead to murder. All over the eastern part of Jersey normal social life for people with young children (among whom I included myself) suddenly came to an end as parents decided to forgo their visits to their local pub or forsake the gay life of the holiday hotels. I and the children suffered as badly as anyone else, our eldest daughter never went anywhere on her own, and this restricted life caused trouble between us.

One of Mannings' first actions was to appeal to every 'man, woman and child' on the island to turn detective. The press was issued with a verbal 'identikit' of the man the police were seeking. He struck always at night and only on moonlit week-ends at this period. He appeared to have an intimate knowledge of the St Martin and St Saviour areas of the island, for nearly all the attacks had taken place there. He invariably wore a low thigh-length jacket of tweedy material (possible a duffle coat) which gave off a distinct, musty smell. Usually he wore a peaked cap and gloves and carried a torch during the attacks which always took place between 10 p.m. and 3 a.m. on Saturday nights and Sunday mornings. His methods followed a distinct pattern; he seemed always to select his victims carefully and appeared to bide his time before striking and his usual method of entry was by a bedroom window. He moved like a wraith for invariably nobody ever heard him until he roused the child he intended to make his victim. These unfortunates were usually blindfolded and then assaulted. In almost every case, a rope was tied round their necks, often being tightened to a point not far from strangulation.

Mannings, working from a room on the second floor of Police H.Q. where a large map of the island hanging on the wall had the sites of 14 attacks pinpointed on it, felt certain the maniac lived in the eastern half of the island for, in particular, he appeared to know every nook and cranny, hedge and footpath in the St Martin's area and had obviously made a careful study of escape routes. He had an uncanny knowledge of every isolated house in the area and when he entered one, appeared to know exactly where to go to – precisely which bedroom was occupied by a child. One he had struck, he used the fields to effect his escape, rarely using a road or lane – although in some cases he appeared to have used a red scooter, stolen from the Grands Vaux area, to make a quick getaway. Local legend had it that he had once been seen to clear a four-foot hedge in a single leap.

In an address to every available policeman, included *centeniers*, *vingteniers* and regular police in St Helier Town Hall on the morning of Saturday, 29th April 1961, Superintendent Mannings urged, 'A local knowledge is a tremendous weapon in this inquiry and we must make full use of it'. An addition to the 'identikit' was that the man spoke good and correct English and used the phrase, 'Jesus' or 'Bejesus'.

Mannings' plan was simple and, so far as it went, effective in that the attacks were to cease over the next two years – although whether the temporary cessation was due to police activity or to the maniac's struggle within himself to prevent Mr Hyde from gaining the upper hand again, is debatable, in view of the fact that attacks had also ceased between 1958 and 1960. Day by day, suspects were hauled into the smart grey-stone Police H.Q. in the Rouge Bouillon where they were interrogated by Mr Mannings and his team. These ranged from every man on the island who had a criminal record, particularly those with a history of sexual offence, to a 47-year-old bearded fisherman called Alphonse le Gastelois, who lived alone in a cottage at St Martin's.

Le Gastelois, unfortunately for him, had a reddish beard and hair – a colour that matched known descriptions of the assailant. He was stocky – about the same height as the suspect; and, living alone and unmarried, also placed himself within the category of those who could be reasonably suspected. Of the thirty two people questioned, le Gastelois offered the most hope to the police. They held him for forty two hours, during which his cottage was searched almost to the point of ransacking and all his clothing was taken away for forensic tests. It was merely the beginning of the ordeal for the poor fisherman; upon his release, he found himself ostracized, for many people were convinced he was guilty. Worse, his cottage was pelted with stones and its windows broken and he was insulted and jeered wherever he was recognized. In despair at the gossip and continued persecution, le Gastelois finally quit Jersey and made a new home for himself on the dangerous reef known as Ecreohus, some eight miles from the island where he settled down to lead the solitary life of a hermit.

Superintendent Mannings also instituted a plan which the press labelled Operation M. This called for a turn-out of all available policemen, both honorary and professional, each week-end. The whole eastern part of Jersey was effectively sealed off by road blocks and foot parties carried out patrols along the narrow lanes and footpaths, particularly in the vicinity of lonely or isolated houses where there were known to be children or young people. Rudie, an Alsatian police dog was flown in from the Staffordshire Training School with his handler, P.C. S. F. Cowie, to help Flash, the only police dog on Jersey, which was handled by P.C. Dick Stokes.

Mannings failed to achieve any really positive results during his short stay on the island however, except possibly to force the maniac to lie low. There were beneficial side effects, of course, particularly a smartening up and reorganization of C.I.D. methods among the Jersey States Police themselves. The Superintendent's efforts also brought to light attacks which had been reported to the honorary police but not passed on to the regular C.I.D. But all his efforts were unable to break through what he and the honorary police considered a 'deliberate conspiracy of silence'. A *centenier* told one newspaper reporter, 'In the small, closely knit communities on the island, there is a reluctance to tell on a neighbour. In fact, many of the people here in country districts are often related. Only by impressing upon them that a child's life may be in danger, have we been able to get co-operation'.

Despite the fact that the Superintendent's plan for sealing off the eastern end of the island every week-end involved putting an enormous strain on the island's police forces, the much-maligned police forces did, in fact, continue with it for over nine months. It was an intolerable strain that could not last; regular policemen were working considerable periods of overtime and the honorary police who were, after all, only on volunteer duty, found it more and more difficult to surrender *all* their week-ends to the hunt. As the weeks lengthened into months and Superintendent Mannings returned to London to his regular duties at Scotland Yard, the plan gradually fell into disuse until, by the end of the year, the flurry of activity had become only a memory.

Helping to damp down the activity, of course, was the knowledge that there had been no more attacks. Compared with the beginning of the year when it seemed as if the maniac, following the phases of the moon, might be planning his attacks on a regular monthly basis, there seemed distinct grounds for optimism. To the C.I.D. who suspected that they might be dealing with a schizophrenic, it seemed as though Dr Jekyll had, at least for the time being, succeeded in expelling Mr Hyde.

It was a calm that was to last only a month short of two years. Then at approximately 1 a.m. on 19th April 1963, yet another sex attack – one for which my husband had been found guilty – was perpetrated against a 9-year-old boy living in Chateau Clairvale in the parish of St Saviour. The boy was sleeping in the nursery bedroom on the ground floor of a house which was isolated and surrounded by trees and hedges. In the same room also lay sleeping his 7-year-old brother.

By some mischance, the ground floor sash-type window had not been fastened. The boy was wakened by a sound near this window; then the window was opened and he saw a torch shining on the carpet. A figure approached him and, as he put it later in evidence before the Royal Court, 'I was very frightened and I hid under the sheets and he went to my brother's bed. He came back to me and then he went back to my brother's bed and did something. I do not know what.' The man had a knife in his hand and warned the boy that if he made a noise to waken his parents, he would murder the parents.

The man took him from his bed and carrying him piggyback, went out through the french-windows, across the lawn and carried him to a field, Clos des Pauvres, normally used for football. He took him into a changing shed and then made him lie down on his side. By this time the boy was crying and Ted Paisnel said, 'Stop crying, or I will cut your throat.'

The charges upon which my husband were eventually found guilty in this case were attempted sodomy and indecent assault. After it was all over, Ted apparently took the boy back into the house and placed him back in his bed, at the same time warning him not to tell his parents what had happened. In a state of shock and fright, the boy remained quiet until he heard a motor-bike start up nearby, then he aroused his parents.

The boy's father, confronted by his son in the parent's bedroom at what appeared to be the middle of the night, at first thought the child had been dreaming until he noticed that the boy was in a dirty state. The mother saw that the boy was terrified but she, too, thought he had been having nightmares until she noticed the mud and earth on him (it had been raining). The moment she saw this, she said later in evidence, 'I thought to myself – this man must be at it again!'

The father, entering the nursery, saw the french-windows, which had been securely locked the night before, lying wide open. There was dirt on the window sill beside the french-windows where the intruder had obviously planted his feet.

The police, on this occasion, were able to add quite a few more significant details to their dossier. Footprints where discovered outside the windows. They were size 8½-9 (Ted's size). Similar footprints were found in nearby flower beds, but they had not been made on the same night which indicated that the intruder had reconnoitred the house some time beforehand (in fact, when the police discovered the hoard of photographs in Ted's secret room, they found one of this house taken at least *three years* earlier; Ted's explanation was that he had had it 'since the war', although evidence was produced to show that the photograph must have been taken between 1957 and 1960). The boy described his assailant as possessing 'glaring eyes' and with bushy eyebrows like white cottonwool. A piece of cottonwool, was in fact, discovered outside the french-windows the next morning by Detective Cockerham (shaped like a false eyebrow and similar to one found by Detective Marsh in Ted's secret room eight years later). The boy also described his assailant's voice 'as a sort of high voice' – 'it was quite cultured – but more of an ordinary worker's voice'. Among the more damning bits of evidence were the seminal stains found on the boys pyjamas which were from a Group O secretor (the boy himself was Group A2; Ted was Group O).

Part of Ted's defence in court was that the boy's mother had 'bought some books from him about two or three years before' – and it was at this time that the photograph of the house had come into his possession. He had 'bought it'. The boy's mother, in evidence, admitted that she had once bought some books from Ted but insisted that 'I don't deal with the labouring classes . . . and I have never entertained him in my house'; and that although she had seen him in St Helier auction rooms, 'I don't make friends with people of his class' – a remark, I fear, which possibly deeply hurt the pride of a man who imagines himself the last of the aristocratic line of the Paisnels.

From the police point of view, one of the most extraordinary aspects of this particular case was the strange illness that befell Flash, the police dog who was, unavailingly, given the task of trying to follow a scent. For two days afterwards, the dog was violently ill; an episode that was to be repeated in 1970 when he was brought in again following another attack on a boy in Vallée des Vaux.

It was near the end of that year – on Sunday, 19th November to be exact – before there was another attack. This again occurred in the parish of St Saviour and again the victim was a boy – an eleven-year-old who was indecently assaulted by a man who climbed up a ladder into his bedroom. The boy could only describe his attacker as being 5 feet 7 inches tall, carrying a black and white torch and wearing dark clothing.

My husband was not charged with this case but on Sunday, 19th July 1964, at 2 a.m., he struck again. This time the assault was on a 10-year-old girl in Trinity parish, in a field adjacent to the rather aptly named La Chasse du Diable.

From Detective Inspector George Shutler's subsequent investigations, there were indications that Ted had had the house under observation for some considerable time; footprints his size were found on the *cotil* at the rear of the house overlooking the girl's bedroom. These same footprints, which were also found on the parquet flooring inside the house, led to the house from Grands Vaux and also went back. Entry had been gained in an ingenious manner. Ted had inserted a broom handle through a kitchen fanlight window, which had allowed him, still using the handle, to reach and release the locking bar on a large window. A thumbprint found on the broom handle matched neither Ted's nor any of the attacked girl's family; but there was a pig-skin scuff on it indicating that he had used pig-skin gloves.

The girl was in the house with her mother and two friends when Ted crept in. He awoke her, told her 'to get out of bed and go downstairs with him.' She thought at first that it was one of her friends. Then he said he had 'some friends downstairs and that I was not to shout because he had a gun'. She went out of the front door with him, then round the back of the house, after first putting on some wellington boots. At the back of the house, she was taken through french-windows into a room where Ted took a rug from the floor and put it around her. She was wearing only her pyjamas and wellington boots. He led her for some 200 yards up the drive and then along a muddy track into a field.

Here he put the rug down on the ground and made her lie on it. Then he lay down alongside her, putting his raincoat over the top to protect her from the rain. He then put a pair of scissors or a knife to her neck and asked her if her father had been in the Navy. She said he had. He then took off her pyjama trousers, blindfolded her and assaulted her. The assault consisted of attempts at normal intercourse and at sodomy.

After the assault, she was taken back to the house. As the blindfold had been taken off and Ted walked on her left side, he insisted that she kept her left eye closed. Back at the house, he told her to go straight upstairs to her bedroom window so that he could see her and be sure that she had gone straight to her room. This the girl did.

The girl identified her attacker as of 'average build', wearing a gabardine raincoat (similar to one taken from Ted's secret room and produced in court) with ridged buttons (similar to those on Ted's raincoat). He had also been wearing gloves with no fingers and a peaked cap (this ,too, was similar to one taken from Ted's secret room). The States Analyst gave evidence that seminal stains on the rug indicated a Group O secretor (Ted's group) and the girl herself was a non-secretor. A pubic hair found on the rug was discovered, under microscopic examination, to be similar to one taken from Ted after his arrest.

One of the intriguing aspects of this case was that during the assault, Ted talked about smoking. In fact, he is a non-smoker and this was only one of the ruses he used from time to time in an effort to throw the police off the scent.

Just over a fortnight later, at 2 a.m. on Bank Holiday Monday, 3rd August 1964. Ted struck again – this time in our own parish of Grouville. It was an area very familiar to him – and, indeed, he had 'borrowed' a car used during a previous attack, from a house near the one he now chose. This time he gained entry by unfastening a kitchen window. He also ate some fruit and stole a vegetable knife from the kitchen drawer.

The boy who was aged 16 and mentally retarded, had got up to go to the toilet when he saw Ted standing in the doorway shining a torch. Ted ordered him back into bed and after warning him to keep quiet or he would kill both him and his parents, had a careful look round the house before following the lad into his bedroom. He then ordered the boy to get out of bed and twisting his arm round his back, led him from the house after again warning him to keep quiet. The lad was forced to walk barefooted and clad only in his pyjamas to a nearby field. Here he was first blindfolded, then spun round to make him lose his sense of direction. Then he was ordered to take off his pyjama trousers and lie on his stomach. When Ted attempted sodomy, the lad began to struggle and Ted then placed a cord round his neck and then a knife at his throat. The boy managed to gasp, 'What happens if the police find you?' and Ted replied quite confidently, 'The police will never find me!'

After the assault, Ted warned the boy to wait ten minutes to allow him to get away. The lad waited two or three, then ran back into the house and roused his father. The father, who had his revolver in a drawer, ran out into the grounds with the avowed intention of killing the assailant if possible. Spotting what seemed to be some movement in the bushes around the house, he opened fire, shooting several bullets but not hitting anyone.

A police search revealed how Ted had entered the house. Also on a window at the rear of the house, a palm print was discovered and under it, a mark or scuff left by pigskin leather. Seminal stains on the boy's pyjamas revealed a Group O secretor and a pubic hair found on the floor of the boy's bedroom not only matched the one found at the scene of the previous assault but once again that taken from Ted after his arrest. This time, however, and very significantly, Ted had changed his voice. The boy found it 'very, very rough' and not like a Jersey accent at all. The police, at the time were thus left with a sex-fiend who variously spoke with an 'Irish' accent, a 'cultured' accent, a 'high' accent and now 'a very very, rough accent.' When a tape recording of Ted's voice, taken from his office after his arrest, was played over to the boy in the Royal Court, the lad had to say, 'It was something like that – but far rougher'. On the other hand, he was able to include in his description of his attacker, the fact that he wore the tell-tale raincoat.

It was time once more to call in Scotland Yard. What now followed became one of the biggest and most thorough police investigations ever carried out in Britain. It was, as one observer noted, far bigger than the average murder hunt – although nobody up till then, had been murdered. Up and down Jersey, however, I should tell you most people believed that the maniac, who had time and again either threatened to kill or, indeed, had sometimes tightened the noose round his victims' necks to such an extent that death lay only a millimetre away, must eventually overstep the mark and actually commit the ultimate crime. To say that Jersey had become an island of fear – at least for those living in rural areas – is not to use an overly-dramatic term.

The day following the Bank Holiday attack Detective Superintendent James Axon (now the Chief Officer of Jersey) accompanied by a sergeant, Leslie Alton, both from Scotland Yard, flew to St Helier and joined forces with the then Chief Officer, Leslie Johnson. There were hopes that the palm print found on a window in the latest case could be matched with the maniac's. One of the first things Superintendent Axon did was to accept an offer made by a local flying club who volunteered to fly him over the scene of every assault. The Superintendent later declared that he had been made dizzy by the deep turns but he had learned a lot.

At least, he saw at once how formidable his task was; there were over 600 miles of road on Jersey and he discovered how easy it is for a man to escape either by road using a scooter or car or by simply running across fields and bisecting roads and thus putting miles between himself and the scene of the crime within a few minutes – certainly long before a hue and cry could be raised. Even if the roads were at once blocked by police cars, the man could easily avoid a cordon. For nine months following Superintendent Mannings visit, foot patrols of honorary and regular police had tramped every lane and footpath in eastern Jersey and yet they had never been able to intercept a suspect. Houses where suspects lived had been kept under 24 hour surveillance during the week-ends; houses in lonely or isolated positions where women or children might be vulnerable had also been kept under observation; yet none of these heavy and sustained operations had yielded a single iota of importance. It was a daunting prospect, no doubt, for the Superintendent as, after landing again, he himself began legging it across the fields and roads in what he possibly hoped might be the footsteps of the maniac, in an effort to find where the various trails would lead. The press at once compared him with Inspector Maigret, Simenon's famous fictional detective and Sergeant Alton, who tore around the roads of Jersey in a car, trying to intercept him, as the faithful Lucas. Axon himself acknowledged that if the criminal were caught, the case would be not only a classic of crime detection but would reveal a background of tangled human emotions that was a story in itself.

Day by day, Axon re-examined every aspect of the case again and again. More than 400 statements were taken and each victim was asked to relate his or her story once more in an effort to unearth some overlooked clue.

Axon, a Scotsman from Edinburgh and described as 'dour, thoughtful and painstaking', had more than a dozen London murder cases behind him before he arrived in Jersey. The biggest task he set himself and the police forces under his control was to fingerprint – or rather palm print – every male between the ages of 19 and 60 living in the eastern end of the island. For weeks lights burned late in Police H.Q. in the Rouge Bouillon. Daily a steady stream of slightly-embarrassed country figures entered C.I.D. quarters, self-consciously bared their arms and then had black ink rolled on to their hands. Each morning, a fresh batch of palm prints were flown to Scotland Yard to be examined by fingerprint experts. Altogether, in the weeks and months that followed, a six-man team managed to take more than ten thousand palm prints and talk to some twenty thousand people. Disappointingly, many of the prints were quite useless – dirt was so engrained in the crevices of men who had spent their lives picking tomatoes that the impressions resulting were mere smudges.

Axon himself worked long and tedious hours. Hundreds of tip-offs, some genuinely intended to be of help, some made maliciously, had the police hareing hitcher and yonger all over the island. Axon himself dug into the records of all the homosexuals on the island and investigated their various backgrounds, on the theory that the maniac had to be a homosexual in view of the nature of his assaults on the boys and the fact that he invariably attempted to use the little girls as boys. It was a view to which I, in particular, subscribed. The Superintendent also spent hours in a field just watching a house where he knew there was a child living – working out exactly what the occupant did and how the maniac might spot his potential victims. He discovered, interestingly enough, that Jersey people living in the country area rarely drew their curtains across at night, which made it relatively easy for an attacker to watch, plot and take his prey.

In a statement to the press, Superintendent Axon declared that he was certain that the maniac – and it seemed likely in view of the stereotyped pattern of the assaults, that there was only one maniac involved – was being shielded by someone. 'A man cannot go out late at night and return in the early hours of the morning, often with mud-stained clothing, without someone noticing. Somewhere a wife or sister or a mother is keeping this man's activities secret.

'If there is someone on the island who has information but doesn't want to talk to the local police, I am prepared to meet them at any secret rendezvous and at any time of the day or night.'

Police activity was spurred by the sense of outrage and indignation sweeping the island, even among people living in St Helier or the other towns on the island who might reasonably consider themselves immune, as the maniac had yet to strike in a built-up area. One expression of this sense of outrage was a reward of £500 offered by the local *Jersey Evening Post*; a sum which was rapidly raised to £1100 as business houses and residents put up other rewards. As no one came forward to claim it, rumour grew; the wanted man was 'wealthy' or the son of a *centenier* and was thus being deliberately shielded.

If the police were getting roughly nowhere with the palm prints they did take, the big operation at least appeared to narrow the field for them. For despite the thousands of palm prints that were collected over some two years, thirteen men stubbornly refused to give their prints. Superintendent Axon and his team steadily went to work on these thirteen men. Some they were able almost immediately to eliminate as suspects; others finally agreed to give a print. At one stage, the number of recalcitrants was reduced to six, a figure that was rapidly reduced to five when it was discovered that one man had been out of the island when some of the attacks took place.

This left only five stubborn Jerseymen who refused to be either coaxed or cajoled into giving their palm prints. It was a not unreasonable assumption that one of these five men was probably the maniac. Finally, of these five, the police felt certain that two of the men could not be guilty – one, for instance, was an ex-policeman. This left three men who adamantly refused to be palm-printed.

The police, in fact, had narrowed the field rather better than they seem to have realized. For among those three – and far the most vociferous in his refusal – was my husband, Ted Paisnel.

SEVEN

A QUESTION OF SUSPICION

Even before I married him, I had realized that Ted Paisnel was an exceptional sort of a person; if you like, perhaps a little odd. Strangely enough, I found the oddities quite appealing; they made me feel he needed mothering.

Even when I had finally seen him at his most violent, I felt an enormous sympathy for him. I realized he had a persecution complex – but I could understand why he had it and feel compassion for him. He seemed to aspire to so much and yet had so little. I thought he had suffered enough in the past and that what he needed most was sympathy and understanding. If I could not give him love after a while, I could at least extend these to him.

Looking back now, I can see a significance about some of the strange things he did that escaped me at the time. For instance, he would never sit down at the table with the rest of us when he ate at home but went off into a corner and ate by himself. It was as though he recognized himself as unclean or felt hunted in some way. Yet when he took us, his small family, out for a meal, his behaviour was perfect.

Whenever he fell ill, he desired no comforting or assistance (yet he could not be more concerned or do more whenever I or any of the children were ill). On these few occasions, he just shut himself up in his room for days and we all learned to leave him alone and never go near him. He did not want help; he merely wanted to be left alone.

The loft in our part of Maison du Soleil adjoins his father's potato loft and there is an opening between the two. On one occasion when we had had a row and I had not seen him for a couple of days, I happened to go up into our loft. To my astonishment, there was Ted next door, sleeping on a dirty old mattress, like a wounded animal nursing its hurts. When he disappeared for a few days – usually after a row (and the rows themselves I now realize, nearly always took place on a Friday), I always imagined that he was sleeping in the loft or some other uncomfortable place. He was a man, after all, for whom the word hardship appeared to have no meaning.

I realized quite early that Ted possessed a vivid imagination (as I thought, a by-product of this lonely childhood) and often tended to live in a world of his own creation; he was, not to put too fine a point on it, a bit of a romancer. There was the time, for instance; when he told us how much he loved playing the guitar; he had owned one, he said, in Wales. For several weeks, we all saved some money so that we could buy him one for his birthday – only to discover that he could, *not* only not play it but had, indeed, never touched one in his life!

He was a superb mimic, of course for there was a strong theatrical element to his personality and he seemed to enjoy changing roles like an actor – dropping his own personality for a while and adopting another. His behaviour on these occasions was always half-comic, half-serious. One can only guess at the various compounds; at the various devious ways his mind was working. Was part of it vanity? A desire to be someone? Was it a simple case of a mind so unstable that it could not fix on a particular personality that suited it, but had to search about?

I am talking, first, about his play-acting. Once, a few years ago, he shaved all his hair off in a Yul Brynner fashion. Had someone told him he resembled Brynner or did he imagine it himself? All I know is that he looked awful. But for weeks he went around happily under the illusion that he looked like the film star. A little later, he went to see John Wayne in a film called 'True Grit'; in this Western Wayne wore a black eyepatch. To my astonishment, one day Ted came in wearing a black eyepatch. 'Who does he think he is now?' I asked one of the children, jokingly.

'John Wayne'.

I can only report that for months afterwards, Ted constantly donned the eyepatch.

It was play-acting of a kind that did not seem really so extraordinary at the time as it might seem now, reading about it in cold print for Ted, as I have said, was a superb mimic. He fell into other people's ways and adopted their voice patterns as easily as a duck sliding into water. If he was with an Irishman he used an Irish accent (which is where the 'Bejasus' or 'Bejabbers' bit came from). If he were with a Cockney, he talked pure cockney, as though born and raised in the East End. He some-

111

times talked like a German – imitating Germans he had known during the Occupation. The police say that they interviewed a man who had once been to Manchester with Ted; he told them that the moment they stepped off the train and began walking along the platform, Ted had already begun talking like a born Mancunian. It was not just a question of accent, either; Ted always got the idiom right. The police were astonished after they had arrested him when Ted began using police jargon as though he had served in the force for years.

Why was I never suspicious, then?

If I had ever stopped to write down on a piece of paper all the oddities and strange facets of Ted's character; if I had combined all these with his various activities, his absences from home, his night prowls; if I had taken all these and, in a sense, *telescoped* them in time, then my suspicions might have been sharply aroused. But this is to ignore that one does not live one's life after this fashion. Day succeeds day in a pattern of, to some extent routine and uniformity. Ted's night rambles, with their perfectly reasonable explanation; his violent outbursts of temper – everything became a *background* to my way of living. Ted and his behaviour ceased to seem all that unusual; one simply got used to it – it was like people who listen to music all day and yet would be hard pressed to name a tune from the hundreds they had heard played.

Nor should it be forgotten that there were very strong pressures operating on the other side. I could not envisage Ted as a highly-sexed man – and I am sure most people, like myself, believed that such a man must be under a particularly strong compulsion (indeed, most of Ted's attacks on children, particularly the later ones, were remarkable in that he seemed to have difficulty achieving his full desires and had to be content with what, in view of his obsession with witchcraft and with the child-murderer, Gilles de Rais, may have been seen by him as a simple ritual or symbolic spilling of the semen). Secondly, I had no doubt (and Mr Axon apparently shared this view) that the assailant was a homosexual) even now, I find *that* about the hardest thing of all to believe about Ted. One may say that I was being too *naive*; that I ought to have known better. I believed, however, that a homosexual was easily recognizable; I had lived in London long enough to know what a queer was and Jersey, after all, was full of them. I still find it a strain on my credulity, despite the court evidence, to see Ted in this light.

It was also asking me to deny the evidence of my own eyes –
Ted's extraordinary way with children. I had seen him ringing a
bell as, dressed up as Father Christmas, he had stood in the drive
of the children's home that first Christmas we met and I had
seen his kindness and gentleness. I had seen him at play with the
children over the years and watched how they responded to
'Uncle Ted'. I knew how marvellous he was with my own
children and all those foster-children who stayed from time to
time at Boulivot. A short while before his arrest, for example,
I took our daughter over to London again to see a specialist.
My mother came with me. After the visit to the specialist we
all went off to Bournemouth for a couple of weeks holidays.
During this time, I left my son with Ted and also a young lad
who was lodging with us. Almost every night, my son and I
would talk on the telephone and I remember his words quite
clearly, 'Oh, don't bother to hurry back, Mum, Dad and I are
having a super time. It's chips and everything – and if we don't
want to cook, he takes me out to the Harvest Barn (a well-known
restaurant). Or we go fishing.' There was Ted alone in the house
with two young lads, yet he never touched them (at the same
time, if I had ever guessed that he was the maniac, is it likely that
I would have left my son alone with him – or, indeed, that I
would have continued to allow foster children to stay at Maison
du Soleil?)'

His attitude towards my elder daughter, too, was more than
enough to lull my suspicions, had any arisen. She was, after all,
merely his step-daughter, there were no ties of blood to interfere with his lascivious desires, if he had had any inclination
that way towards her. He watched her grow from a child into a
pretty young woman (she is married now); he watched her stride
about the house in a bra and brief panties and I never saw his
eyes rest on her attractive figure for a moment. He would not
even raise his head from a newspaper or book. A man less likely
to be plagued by sexual desires it would seem impossible to
find.

Nor does any of this overlook the sheer guile displayed by
Ted. I have mentioned some of the ways he tried to throw the
police off the scent by dropping false clues – the different voices,
particularly the Irish voice, which was intended to make the
police suspect seasonal workers; the remark that his mother was
dead; the talk about the Navy; his talk about smoking and his
search for his 'lighter'. Later, he would deliberately drop a glove

in a driveway – a glove he had picked up somewhere and which he knew could not be traced back to him, but which would have the police hareing off on yet another false scent. As Det/Inspector George Shutler has said, 'Make no mistake, Ted Paisnel was a clever blighter'.

So far as I was concerned, he did everything he could to allay any suspicions I might ever have had. My son, for example, always slept downstairs with my foster children for we had an alarm connected to my room; once the attacks had started again, Ted was most solicitous. 'Now, I want you to put the terriers out tonight, just in case' and then, as an additional safeguard, he insisted that the children ceased sleeping downstairs and were given a small room upstairs, next to mine.

He worked himself into an even greater lather of concern about my elder daughter. She often cycled home alone from a dance or from meeting her boy friend, although once the attacks had started up again, her boy friend (whom she has now married) always took good care to walk her the whole way home. Ted, however, would come bursting into my room, saying 'It's gone eleven and Chrissie's not home. You don't know what might happen to her along those roads'.

'Oh, she'll be all right' I'd say.

'Come on,' he'd insist.

'Well, let's give it another five minutes. You know I can't leave the baby.'

'No, come on, *now*,' he would demand, almost beside himself, 'You wait five minutes and anything could happen. There's this man at large – we're not free in this island.'

On several occasions, he forced me to get up out of bed and then, both of us in our dressing gowns, drive down the lanes until we met her happily swinging along, hand in hand with her boy friend.

It is comforting to believe that, perhaps, under the influence of the moon, he was not responsible for what he was doing; even, that he did not fully comprehend what he was doing. His concern *might* have been genuine, in the sense that he knew that when in the grip of his compulsion, he could easily attack any lone woman. I try hard to think of him this way, but I have to admit that all the evidence is against me. The police point out that he planned almost every attack like a professional criminal; that he would wait years to break into a house he had already marked down. They see him as going about the island on his business as a builder, working on one house while keeping the house next door under surveillance; then months, years later, striking in the night.

Nor can I forget his feigned indignation when yet another attack would be reported in the local paper. I remember how his face turned white, his hands clenched and he would declare, 'They should lynch him when they get him!' His reactions were always those natural to a man who was father to a family and in whose care lay the well-being of several small children (I am including the foster children).

His protective attitude did not end there. I never thought of Ted as being a particularly brave man but I remember one night when the attacks were at their height, my daughter coming home and telling me, 'Mummy, there's a strange man in the field opposite, looking up our drive.' The man next door had two young girls, so we were all very much on edge at the time. I called Ted and told him there was a strange man kneeling behind the hedge and watching either our house or the one next door.

Ted at once shot out of the house and launched an attack on the man. They had a terrible fight. The man ran off to where his car was parked in a lane. Ted chased him and got hit over the head with a potato box, and the man escaped. Naturally, we called the police and Ted told them that the man had escaped 'in a blue Ford'. We were all asked to describe him and the police got very excited when we said he looked 'like Stirling Moss' – because among the descriptions they had of the sex-fiend was one that said he had a very high forehead.

The police, in fact, were pretty smart on this occasion and eventually tracked the man down. He turned out to be a French farm worker who couldn't speak a word of English. He claimed all he had been doing was urinating behind the hedge. Ted was called as a witness, but his behaviour in court was, to put it mildly, very strange. He was extremely nervous and could hardly answer a question. He made a laughing-stock of the whole proceedings, claiming, 'It was really nothing, sir, the man was just looking at our house and my wife and mother got a bit hysterical, so I tackled the man and got a tap on the head.'

'You mean it was just a case of a punch-up between two men because the women got hysterical?'

'That's all, sir,' said Ted.

'This is just wasting my time,' declared the magistrate and dismissed the case.

Since Ted's arrest the man is said to have explained his behaviour to the detectives by claiming 'I was told that there was a black magic circle up at Boulivot and that there were women dancing naked round the house.'

He was an extraordinary mixture, really, was Ted. I am thinking now of the simple domestic pursuit of watching T.V., for instance. I can recall one family Christmas when they were showing a rather poignant film on T.V. I remember turning to look at him when the film ended, only to find his eyes moist with tears.

Sex on T.V. annoyed him intensely. When a play was performed showing intimate scenes, he would either get up and turn off the set or rise and leave the room. Nor did he think it proper for the children to watch tentative love-making on the box. On the question of violence, however, he and I differed markedly in our view. I considered that there was little harm in allowing the children to learn something of 'the facts of life', but I took exception to violent scenes, for I think violence is the greater of the two problems. I tended to turn off the T.V. set when there was violence, which upset Ted. 'You're too puritanical!' he used to shout at me. 'You've got to let the children learn what life is all about! There's violence in life as well as love!'

He continually confounded me by his actions – to such a degree, I suppose, that I refused to take a lot of things he said or did too seriously. One day, for instance, a man came to me and said, 'Here's the account Ted asked for?' The man was a garage owner and the account concerned petrol and repairs to the car.

'What's this for?' I asked, for Ted didn't usually ask for an account.

'Oh, he's closing his account.'

'Why, what for?'

'He's joining the Foreign Legion, didn't you know?'

'No, I didn't and I think he's having you on.'

'No, no. He's quite serious.'

'It's a leg pull,' I insisted.

'Well, he's going all over the island settling his accounts. He says he's going to France – and going to join the Legion.'

This turned out to be the first – and last – I ever heard about *that* subject.

The police believe that Ted got rid of a certain amount of incriminating evidence by burning it. If he did, he was very clever

116

about it. Certainly, he burned a lot of stuff about the house, but one would have had to be very suspicious and something of an amateur detective to ready anything much into what he did. He certainly used to burn a lot of stuff in the sitting-room grate. I would say something like, 'The fire's getting low – will you throw a few more bits of coal or bits of wood on.'

Grumbling after the usual fashion of a husband disturbed in the middle of his favourite T.V. programme, Ted would say, 'Oh, all right, I suppose I'd better go and get something.'

He would got off into the night, only to return five or ten minutes later with bits of old wood, rubbish of all descriptions and pairs of boots or shoes and bits of clothing. Inevitably, such a collection aroused a terrible stink and I would protest vigorously.

'It's all I could find' he would say.

On other occasions, he would tell the children, 'I've got a real treat for you tonight. I've got a lot of rubbish – so we'll have a bonfire!'

He always told me it was rubbish he had collected from his customers – old bits of fencing, rubbish from gardens, all sorts of building rubbish and debris; he would drive up with cartloads of this sort of rubbish every so often. Then that evening, with the kids rushing round with squeals of delight, Ted would light a big bonfire in the field at the back of the house. If he burned incriminating boots or clothing, how on earth was I supposed to know?

There were, of course, many clues there if I had been a suspicious wife – or an amateur detective. I have told you of the kind of books Ted read. There were works of palmistry, astrology, astronomy, hypnotism, philosophy, literature, poetry – on any subject you care to mention. From his prison cell he has asked to be supplied with the following books: *The Life Divine*, by Sri Aurobindo; *The Supreme Doctrine*, by Hubert Benoit; *Buddhism*, by David-Neel; the books of Gurdjieff; *Joyful Wisdom* by Nietzsche; all the works of Ouspensky; *Venture with Ideas*, by K. Walden; all the books of T. Lobsang Rampa; *Notes of a Native Son*, by Jes Baldwin; *Chronicles of a Life* by Siegfried Trebitsch and *The Poetic Image* by Cecil Day Lewis, the late Poet Laureate; an indication of the extraordinary range of his reading and interests. He rarely, if ever, read what is called a 'popular' newspaper and always preferred the type known as 'heavies' or 'qualities'; in prison, he insisted on the *Daily Telegraph* which, according to a letter he has written from gaol, makes him the first prisoner who ever asked for it, and the wonder of his fellow inmates.

Yet he was almost as fascinated by horror comics. These were cheap paperback affairs made up of melodramatic drawings with balloon captions with spidermen about to ravish some almost totally naked girl. The hero, sometimes armed with an iron glove possessed of such sophisticated technological properties that it could not only fire a death-dealing ray but make the wearer invisible if he chose was, inevitably, a super-hero who made James Bond look stupid. I have no doubt that in the recesses of his disturbed mind, my husband often identified himself to some extent with these ridiculous supermen heroes.

I detested these comics and protested when he brought them into the house. If he left them lying around, I simply took them and stuffed them into the Aga cooker in the kitchen. He always explained sheepishly that he hadn't actually bought the comics himself, but that they had been given to him by the 'old boy' – meaning his father. I insisted that these were not the kind of publications that ought to be left lying around where impressionable young children might see them and be influenced by them. Ted would murmur something about 'Puritanical Joan' and leave it at that.

I think it was around 1964 that I first heard a rumour that Ted had been carrying on with other women. I mentioned the rumour about one young woman to my daughter and she dismissed it immediately: 'Oh, don't be silly, mummy, Ted's far too fussy to go with her – he's a very fussy man, you know.' Until that point, I had never given much thought to the idea that Ted might be unfaithful. I believed he still loved me and that he led a celibate life; I used to feel a little sorry for him, thinking, 'Poor devil, what does he get out of life – slaving seven days a week and looking after all of us and living there on his own.' I was disturbed when I first heard about the matter; the idea of divorce did cross my mind, but then I realized that it was unreasonable to expect a man to remain faithful under the circumstances. Neither of us could see any advantage in a divorce. Ted was happy to have a good home and a family around him and he had no intention of marrying any of the women he was meeting. I, for my part, after I had got over my initial surprise felt contented enough with the arrangement; Ted provided me with a home, cared for and nurtured my children and enabled me to carry on my fosterage work.

I was a little surprised, all the same, when the big drive to have all the men in the eastern part of Jersey palm-printed resulted in a stubborn refusal by Ted to co-operate.

'Why not?' I demanded of him.

'I'm a Jerseyman, that's why. And it's a Jerseyman's right to refuse to be fingerprinted.'

He pointed out that there were thirteen other men (at this time) who had refused to be fingerprinted. 'We're Jerseymen – and we know our rights.'

I was vaguely aware that Jersey had these old laws and customs that were very different from Britain's and, to start with, I dismissed his refusal as just another example of Jersey stubbornness. Living with Ted, I had become aware how much these half-Frenchmen resented British 'interference' and I really thought that this was just another example of this resentment. I tried to plead with him that by refusing to be palm-printed, he was laying himself open to suspicion.

He merely shrugged.

'There are a whole lot of respectable Jerseymen as well as me and none of us will be fingerprinted – we know our rights. Besides, they already have my fingerprints.'

'What do you mean?'

'When I was jailed for a month during the German Occupation. My fingerprints were taken then. They have them already. Let them look for them!'

At the time, it all seemed so innocent and so reasonable.

EIGHT

NEAR MISS

It may be that Ted Paisnel was struggling with himself; struggling fiercely with his *alter ego*; it could be, on the other hand, that police activity remained so intense for a while that even he was deterred. The evidence suggests the former, for it is clear that in his vanity, he was certain he could outwit the police.

The year 1966 was remarkable in Ted's case for four things in my mind. First, after a two year interval, there was another savage sex attack. Second, on the last day of the year, there was a brutal murder of a Finnish au pair girl. Third, there was the night when the police surrounded our house at three o'clock in the morning, having just failed to trap Ted. Fourth, there were the bitter arguments between Ted and me about his continuing refusal to be palm-printed. It was also the year that Ted wrote his boastful letter to the police, claiming that he intended committing the 'perfect crime'; although, at the time, I was not aware that he was the writer.

Police activity had fallen away by the late summer of 1966. The searches, the patrols, the cordons, the palm-printing, the interviewing (nearly 30,000 people altogether were interviewed by the police) had lessened to such an extent, indeed, that there were periods when it had almost ceased. Detective Superintendent James Axon had returned to Scotland Yard after spending six months in Jersey. A request by the regular police that two C.I.D. men should be permanently seconded to duties connected *only* with tracing the sex-fiend, were, I understand, turned down on the grounds that the establishment was under-manned as it was and that there were not enough men to spare. The *centeniers* and *vingteniers* continued to give their services, particularly at weekends, but as month succeeded month and the patrols proved fruitless, they were either diverted or diverted themselves to other duties. The hunt never quite died away but the hue and cry fell to a much lower level.

On Saturday, 6th August 1966, the hunt was suddenly up again. A 15-year-old girl who that night, had gone as she did every Saturday evening, to The Place, a dance hall in Providence Street, St Helier, was the victim. Usually, she caught a bus near her home in Trinity parish, north of The Town (as St Helier is always called in Jersey) and joined two girl friends. When the dance finished, just after 11 o'clock, she usually caught the bus home, accompanied by her two friends or was given a lift by her sister and her boy-friend. On this night, she took the bus.

The bus dropped her off near her home at about 11.45 p.m. She reached the drive of her house safely enough, at the entrance to which were some bushes. As she began walking up the drive she heard a voice coming from the bushes telling her to stand still and not to make a noise. Instead, she screamed, involuntarily dropped a birthday card given to her by her boy friend and ran. She had not got very far when she suddenly felt a shove and tripping over the grass verge at the edge of the drive, she fell. Then 'a man got on top of me and I screamed'.

Her plight was quite a scarifying one. The man gripped her by the throat and began choking her so that she could not breathe. She tried desperately to push him away or claw his hands away. It was useless. For what 'seemed quite a long time' he kept his hands tight round her neck, scarcely allowing her to breathe. He kept warning her not to scream. When satisfied that he had subdued her, he finally took his hands away from her throat. Then with a bit of cord, he tied her hands together, in such a way that they were behind her neck. Although she wanted to scream, she was still unable to, as she was fighting to get her breath back. Ted (he was convicted in this case) pulled her up and tried to make her walk. She stumbled several times and kept bumping into him. Her eyes had become accustomed to the dark by now and she could see that he was wearing wellington boots with the tops turned down and had dark trousers tucked into them.

Ted, according to her account, led her into a field. Here he left her for a moment while he walked off alone up the field, presumably to reconnoitre. As she put it herself, she 'began to stagger away' when Ted returned and warned her ominously, 'I told you not to do anything stupid.'

His next remark totally terrified the girl.

'Do you know how long it takes to kill a woman – five minutes'.

She was made to strip; her ankles were tied together; and a cord or belt put round her neck and tightened. Then she was raped.

When it was all over, the girl waited for a while before plucking up the courage to ask if she could go home? Ted agreed to let her go but warned her to wait until she heard a car moving away and on no account 'to call the coppers'. He then left her and, after a few minutes while she listened for the sound of a car but heard nothing, she finally made a dash for her home. She was on her way up her own drive again when she heard a car approaching and frightened that it was her attacker coming back, she started running away again. Then she heard the voices of her sister and her aunt who had come out in her father's car to look for her.

She was able to furnish a pretty precise description of her assailant. He was 'aged about 40, of medium build and medium height, wearing a gabardine mac and a belt with a buckle that jingled. He spoke in a husky voice with a Jersey accent.'

Seen next day by Dr David N. M. Scott, the doctor found that her injuries were consistent with her story that she had been assaulted and then raped in a field near her home. There were marks on her ribs and ankles consistent with her being tied and, in fact, there were marks all over her body. One of the most frightening aspects of the attack were that if the ligature round her neck had been maintained much longer, she would have certainly lost consciousness and the result could have been fatal.

For the first time in any of the cases, strange scratches were found on the victim's naked torso. The doctor was puzzled at the time by these scratches on the girl's back for they were spaced apart quite regularly – and were long scratches. He thought it highly unlikely that they could have been caused by brambles or ordinary barbed wire or even fingernails. Only when he was shown Ted's wristbands of nails did he see something that could be the consistent cause of the scratches. When he examined the nails, he found traces of human blood on them.

It was sometime about three o'clock in the morning of 7th August – three and a quarter hours after the girl had first heard the man call to her from the bushes in her driveway – that I was awakened by a hammering on the door downstairs and the noise of men milling about below in the lane and courtyard.

There are three bedrooms on the second floor at Maison du

Soleil – mine is at the end, the children next to mine and Ted slept in the far bedroom.

Shaken out of my sleep and wondering if the world had come to an end, I got out of bed and went over to the window and raised it. I looked out and saw all these policemen milling about below. Very significantly, they were led by Centenier le Brun, which meant that they had full authority to arrest anyone.

'What on earth's wrong?' I shouted.

'Is that Mrs Paisnel?'

'Yes, what's the matter?'

'Where is your husband, Mrs Paisnel?'

'I don't know – in bed, I suppose. Why?'

'Isn't he in bed with you?'

'No – he sleeps in his own bedroom.'

'Has he been in all night?'

'Yes – at least, so far as I know.'

'He doesn't sleep in the same room as you, then?'

'No. . . . '

I don't suppose that my answers were all that coherent; they never are, are they, when one is woken up suddenly in the middle of the night? Anyway, I was doing my best to gather my scrambled wits together when suddenly the window two rooms away shot up and Ted's wrathful face shot out.

'What the hell's going on down there?' he demanded in an angry voice. 'Get off these premises at once or I'll set the dogs on you. What the devil do you mean coming around here at this hour of the morning, wakening my family up like this. Clear off!'

'Just a minute, Mr Paisnel?'

'What is it?'

'Have you been in all evening – or have you just got in?'

'I've been in all bloody evening!' exploded Ted. 'Now will you get off this property!'

I didn't hear the rest of the exchanges. There was a lot of angry shouting from Ted and what appeared to be explanations from the *centenier* and the police. Then they went away. I went out on to the landing and Ted came out of his room. To my astonishment, he was fully dressed. He had on his woolly Norwegian fisherman's cap and the windcheater he wore under his raincoat.

'What on earth's all that about?' I asked him.

'There's been another attack' he said.

'But why on earth should they call on *you*?'

'They say that it's because I've refused to be fingerprinted – that whenever there's an attack now, they start checking on all the men who've refused to be fingerprinted.'

'And where've you been?' I insisted. 'Look at you. You're fully clothed; you haven't been to bed – and look at the state you're in.' He was all wet and muddy and covered in grass seeds.

'I've been fishing – that's where I've been. You know I always go poaching in the valley. I was coming home when I ran into all this lot – there was a cordon out. I had to make my way over the fields because I didn't want to be picked up.'

'Why, what difference would that have made?'

'They'd have caught me for poaching. I'd have been summoned and had my name in the paper – I don't want *that*.'

He sounded terribly convincing and certainly the indignation he had directed against the police had all the hallmarks of an innocent man. To say that I was suspicious would be to put it much too strongly, but I can say that I did check his story about the fish. It was not that I disbelieved him; it was just an unconscious desire to check in order to be reassured. Sure enough, down in the kitchen was this bucket full of trout. Whatever else he had been doing that dreadful night, he had also been fishing. Even now when I think of it, I'm thunderstruck at the guile of the man!

'Listen, love' he said, when I had gone back upstairs again, 'the police are bound to be back again in the morning. If they do ask you – stick to the story; I was in all night. Otherwise, the whole thing about poaching will come out and I'll find myself in court.'

It was impossible not to accept his explanation. I complained again that he ought to be fingerprinted, but I got the same answer as before; he was a Jerseyman and it was a Jerseyman's right to refuse and anyhow, they had already got his prints.

I have often been asked: Was I *never suspicious*? There have been suggestions, indeed, that following this episode, I *knew* Ted was the sex-fiend and that I actually told someone. Indeed the police received an anonymous letter saying I *believed* my husband to be the guilty man.

This was a totally wrong interpretation of what I had said and believed. Following the attack on the girl at Trinity, a description published in the local paper said that the man had 'rough hands'. Earlier descriptions of the attacker had said that he had 'a prickly moustache' and that he had fair or sandy hair. I happened to be talking to my woman cleaner one day when the question of the attacks arose. We were discussing the descriptions published and more in the sense that these could be applied to all sorts of men, I remarked, 'Oh, isn't it awful – it could be either of our husbands.'

Naturally I tried to think of anyone I knew who was homosexual or 'strange' with children from time to time as I am certain did every wife, sister and mother in the island. As I have said before, if I had sat down and made a list of the 'suspicious' circumstances, I might well have been driven to the conviction that he was guilty. Shortly after we were married and when there had been an attack, I remember he told me that his mother's brother had pulled a girl off a cycle many years ago and had assaulted her and had been put away. He led me to understand, however, that it was a 'frame-up' by certain relatives anxious to make sure that the fellow did not share in an inheritance. To be truthful I never paid much attention to this cock-and-bull story – the Paisnels always seemed such a strange family and one was constantly caught up in a maze of romancings, exaggerations, superstition and illusions of grandeur.

I suppose it was the idea of 'rough hands' more than anything else that prompted my remark. I remember saying to the cleaner, 'Ted has terribly rough hands after he has been using cement'. Cement, in fact, made his hands like sandpaper. If he touched any clothing, you could hear the rasping sound – his hands were so rough. Indeed, he used to rub zambuck into his hands when he had been using it. To my mind, however, far from pin-pointing Ted as the criminal, the 'rough hands' merely meant that it might be any man who laboured with his hands.

We had many quick quarrels around this time, however, concerning his refusal to give his palm-prints. Two days after the attack on the girl at Trinity, Det/Superintendent Axon returned to Jersey – this time as the new Chief Officer of the regular police; a position he still holds. Such was the panic aroused by the latest attack that Mr Axon took up his position six days earlier than he was officially supposed to. The drive to complete the palm-printing was renewed. The local newspaper printed a warning, telling parents not to allow their children to remain out late at night or return home unaccompanied. All over the island, people went to bed only after they had securely fastened all windows and doors; even then, they slept with a sense of fear, for the ability of the beast of Jersey to gain entrance to a house with all the skill of a cat-burglar had now become well-known. Some men bought shotguns; one woman slept with a revolver under her pillow.

We had a really big row about the palm-printing early in the New Year. This followed the brutal murder of a Finnish au pair girl Tuula Hoeoek, aged 20, whose battered body was discovered in a field in St Clement parish on New Year's Eve. Once more the *centenier* and the police called on us, asking Ted to give his palm prints. Again he refused. They explained that they were investigating a murder. Yet he still refused. When the police had left, we had a row about it.

'Why don't you give your prints?' I demanded. 'So long as you don't, suspicion will fall on you every time something happens.' I reminded him of what had happened to Alphonse le Gasteloi who had been driven out of his home when suspicions were aroused about him.

'I've told you – the police already have them,' he insisted.

'They say they no longer have them.' (Fingerprints taken during the German Occupation were believed to have been destroyed, but, in fact, eventually turned up in an old storeroom in Police H.Q. after Ted had been arrested.)

'Well, that's up to them. If they think I've done something wrong – then let them charge me. Otherwise I'm not giving my fingerprints.'

'Why, why not? If only to remove suspicion?'

'All right, then, I'll tell you why.'

His explanation was that he had been once a member of the Communist Party and had defected. This resounded quite reasonable to me because I knew from his talk that he had extreme Left Wing views (following his arrest, he talked to the police quite a lot about his Communist convictions). His worry was – or so he claimed – that if Soviet Russia invaded France and the Channel Islands were taken over by the Communists, then he would be shot as a defector. They would be able to trace him through his fingerprints.

That sounds like the cock and bull story it is, I know. But one had to know Ted, to know the way his mind worked, to see the daft logic of it all. It is to take no account, if one disputes it, of the way Ted used to talk about things. One minute he would be talking about Buddhism; the next about Communism; the

126

next about black magic; the next about philosophy; the next about some building job – every subject under the sun, in fact. I suppose the range of his interests and the variation in his experiences, from working with the Germans, to living in France, to going down a coal mine, to tickling trout and lifting sleeping birds out of their nests in the hedges, really meant that nothing he said or did really surprised me. Back of all my feeling and attitudes, too, was the sincere conviction that the maniac could not be anything like Ted. To start with, he would be a blatant homosexual. He would not be the sort of man who could be genuinely kind to children and be loved by them. Essentially, he would be a callous and cruel man. Even now, I have a terrible battle to convince myself sometimes that the police have not got the wrong man. I know this is crazy and illogical; it shows I have little knowledge of the mentality of a schizophrenic.

The murder of the Finnish au pair girl, when we heard about it, seemed one with the rest of the sex attacks carried out by the maniac although there have been two sex murders in Jersey within the past decade for which other people have been convicted.

At the time, the police apparently desperately desired to trace a blue car or van in which the unfortunate girl was assaulted and battered to death before her body was left in the field. Every owner of a blue car or van on the island was interviewed and every blue vehicle carefully checked. Every blue vehicle except one, that is – Ted's. The explanation as to why Ted was never approached nor his van checked is amazingly simple and in no way reflects discredit on the police. They carefully catalogued every blue vehicle on the island *according to the registration records* and patiently and with great perseverance tracked down every owner and every vehicle in Jersey. It was Ted's habit, however, to purchase his vans second-hand from the Jersey Marketing Board and his van was listed in the records as brown. Ted, *however*, repainted it so that it matched everything else he owned – blue. Following his arrest, I was told he took great delight in telling the police about his blue van. They at once came out to interview me and I told them what I knew about it. Yes, Ted had once owned an old blue van. Yes, he stopped using it – in fact, he left it lying in a field at the back of the house so that the children could play in it. When they got fed up with it, he got a welder to cut it up into little pieces – he didn't want to pollute the environment by leaving bits of old scrap metal lying about in a field. What had happened to the bits ? – he'd given them to a man who was dumping litter on to a site which he wanted to raise to a new level and build upon.

I know that the police drove down to the dump to see what they could find. The dump had risen several feet since 1967 and the police knew it would be quite impossible to recover enough of the bits to reconstruct the van in anything like its entirety again.

The police interviewed me later at great length, in particular asking me if I could remember where Ted had been that particular New Year's Eve. It had been a trying year, I could remember, for Ted and I had had constant rows about the finger-printing. Conditions between us had become so bad, indeed, that I thought the marriage might break up completely and I took the children and myself off up to the Home for a while. Ted was very upset, however, and did everything he could to try and bring us back. He came every Sunday to collect the children and bring them out. He redecorated the whole of the house, even down to buying special curtaining from a Lancashire textile company and he put teddy bear wallpaper in the children's rooms. He really worked hard, day and night to make Maison du Soleil very nice until I finally agreed to go back for a few days to see how we got on again.

This was in November, 1966 and I agreed to stay on when I saw all he had done. We had a reasonably happy Christmas, as I recall, although as usual I got sick – I always seem to get sick at Christmas. When we come to the critical New Year's Eve – well, Ted had a mood that night and went out in a huff about something; so far as I knew he went to his parents next door. It made little difference – in fact he never spent a New Year's Eve with me. I was always alone.

The next day – New Year's Day, that is – there is an entry in my new 1967 diary; 'Ted and I and the children had a lovely walk on Archirondel beach today and he picked some spinach. A beautiful day, warm and sunny. A good start perhaps to the new year ?'

This was the morning after the murder – a particularly brutal murder – of the poor Finnish girl. Because of his other crimes, Ted has naturally become a suspect in this case but I find it hard to believe that a man who could perpetrate such a bloody murder – and apparently it was only too literally a bloody murder – could romp and play with his children and all our little foster children on Archirondel beach the following day without, seemingly, a care in the world or without the slightest trace of guilt or remorse.

Detective/Inspector Shutler has told me that I and my family were probably the safest family on the island; that whatever compelled Ted to do what he did would never have caused him to turn on his own. Like a wild beast who ravaged far and wide, he would never befoul his own lair.

This may well be so and it is an attractive enough theory. So far as I am concerned, however, if I had ever really suspected that Ted Paisnel was the beast of Jersey, I would have started running – and probably would not have stopped yet. Even now, I shudder when I think of the risks run by our foster children over the years – both at the children's home and at Maison du Soleil. Even if my children could be said to be 'safe', what about the innumerable foster-children who have been in the care of my mother and myself since 1953? One of the most melodramatic aspects of this exceedingly melodramatic tale, in my opinion, is this curious juxtaposition – a Beast who ravaged little children living in a privileged position amid so many tiny children.

Dozens of questions have been put to me not only by the police but by reporters and others. For instance, did it never occur to me that Ted *could* be the guilty man?

The answer is that I was concerned not because I thought he was the man but that he might get taken to the station under suspicion because of his roaming about and because of the affair of the fingerprints, and that as a result he might suffer the same humiliation and publicity as Alphonse le Gauloise, and so would we his family. If I had believed I was in the home of a monster does anyone think I could really continue to have stayed there? Even if I had been prepared to submerge my suspicions *on my own account* (although it is hard to see what profit, in any sense of the word, there was in it for me), can it be supposed that I would have risked the life or well-being of the little children placed under my care? Some nights, for example, I left my own and three foster-children in the care of this beast while I went off to my Women's Institute or some other social engagement. I would call over the inter-com to Ted, 'Can you baby-sit tonight, Ted? – I've got a meeting in Town?' I can envisage no circumstances under which I could have behaved like this, if I had for one moment ever suspected Ted Paisnel.

What about the old fawn raincoat? Ted wore a variety of old

clothes during his working hours – after all, the job of building contractor is not one that a man dresses up for in top hat and tails? I was used to seeing his wearing the raincoat, tied round the middle with a bit of cord.

'That looks awful' I remember telling him once. 'Why do you wear that old coat – and in that way too?'

'I don't want it billowing about – that's why I tie the cord round me.'

'You could wear a belt, couldn't you?'

Ted would merely shrug and mumble something and I would let the matter drop. After all, a labouring man, working with bricks, cement, tiles and all sorts of stuff, cannot be expected to be too particular. Since then, I have been told that he wore the cord round his middle (which bunched the raincoat up) as part of his black magic symbolism. I have also learned that he engraved the sign of the fish in any stonework he carried out, because it was the emblem of the monks of the Chapel of the Holy Innocents – the beautiful church attached to his castle, upon which Ted's great hero, Gilles de Rais, lavished immense sums of money.

The police have told me that in their search for the Beast of Jersey over the years, they were convinced that the man they sought would either 1) be a bachelor, or 2) a married man living apart from his wife. Ted Paisnel certainly came within the 'frame' of their suspects once he refused to be palm-printed and again when they discovered that although he still lived in the same house as I did, we no longer shared the same bedroom. I, of course, was never privy to these suspicions and my attitude was that Ted probably did some philandering on the side – after all, sex is not difficult for men to find. Nor, as we had ceased to have relations for some time, was I in a position to censure him. The idea, when he disappeared or stayed out late, that he might be with a woman often occurred to me.

It was in 1968 that Ted met Florence Hawkins who was to remain his self-confessed mistress up until his arrest. Florence came from Salford, Lancashire and was 45-years-old when she met Ted and, according to her own account, still a virgin; Ted, in fact, she says was the first man she ever allowed to make love to her.

Our London committee had sent Florence as an auxiliary nurse or assistant house-mother at the Home. It seems a friendship sprung up between herself and Ted when he gave her lifts to and from St Helier and after chance meetings in the evening, when she was out walking her dog, Bobbie, they strolled together and he told her of his 'unhappy marriage', mentioning 'Goddess Joan', meaning me. As the friendship warmed, they walked together round the coastal cliffs or met in out of the way little tea-shops. Eventually, while they sat together on an island near one of the reservoirs, Ted kissed her and the friendship eventually ripened into intimacy.

Although Florence herself was an excellent worker, my mother had become exasperated with the behaviour of her dog, Bobbie. It barked all day and was a thorough nuisance. Then my mother discovered that Florence was seeing Ted. She remonstrated with her, insisting that it wasn't right. Florence answered, 'I can't help it – he's such a nice man'. This, together with the dog's behaviour was enough to cause my mother to dismiss her. Florence then got a job as auxiliary nurse in the Jersey General Hospital and moved into an annexe to premises owned by a Mr Berger in Savile Street, St Helier. Berger is well-known on the island as an antique merchant and dealer in rare books on all subjects, including philosophy, astrology, palmistry and witch-craft. Ted 'borrowed' some of Mr Berger's books, including, I understand, the copy of *The Black Baron* found in Ted's library by the police the day they discovered the secret room.

Ted, I understand, helped Florence in her move and did up her new room and it was there, according to her own account, that she and Ted made love for the first time the day after she moved in. She has described him as a sensitive and gentle lover. He visited her regularly every Saturday evening when they listened to the radio – he loved good music – or just sat talking. Sometimes they made love.

They made love with more regularity every Sunday morning while lunch was cooking on the gas cooker. Both were vegetarians, and the meal was always a vegetarian one. Ted apparently was very proud of his sexual prowess and could 'satisfy' her twice within the hour. She learned that he had had many other women, but it seems he never bragged about his conquests. She found him essentially 'a quiet man'. Sometimes they changed the venue and she came out to Boulivot where they made love in his bed-sitter – which he had built, according to her, 'as a retreat from the constant quarrelling with his wife, Joan.'

She has admitted that she knew about Ted's secret room, but claims that she never saw the objects found in it. As for the 'black magic' altar, she gave the china toad to him herself, she insists, having bought it in a gift shop. She thought him a 'bit of a weirdie' so far as black magic was concerned, for it was true, in her opinion, that he did have a different side of his character – 'a side that was obsessed with dark affairs of the occult'. He once asked her if she had ever taken any interest in black magic and then explained it to her and showed her some books on the subject. She herself never took part in any black magic orgies, however, and remained impressed with Ted's love of nature. She also found it impossible to believe that this 'kind, sensitive man whose "rough hands" stroked her body like silk,' could be the Beast who terrorized Jersey for at least eleven long years.

NINE

EXCURSION INTO BLACK MAGIC

The existence of black magic circles on the island of Jersey is a matter that is common knowledge, but because of their secretive and shadowy nature and the natural fear that is aroused by the very mention of them, it is an existence that is quite impossible to prove in a Court of Law. I know that following Ted's arrest, the police tried to unearth such a circle and the local T.V. station carried out a fairly thorough independent investigation. Both investigations produced plenty of gossip, but nothing of a more substantial nature.

The police asked a writer on black magic subjects if he were able to interpret Ted's 'altar' and the various articles found there. He replied that they were entirely consistent with the practice of black magic. They also consulted an acknowledged expert in black magic whose name has not been disclosed. His observations were of such a nature that the police were left in no doubt that Ted was involved in black magic – although he himself, in letters from prison to his mother, has denied that he was 'a Satanist.'

The expert explained that every witch or warlock possesses a ritual knife or tool. The 'highest' form of knife, usually, is one with some silver on it – because of the 'purity' of silver. When told that Ted possessed a knife or 'cross' of wood, the expert, according to the police 'almost jumped out of his chair'. 'That means he has gone very, very far', he said, because wood was the 'purest' of all. His comments on the other subjects confirmed their black magic symbolism. The cloves were a 'good luck' charm. The chalice ? – 'he hoped they hadn't drunk anything out of it'. His findings confirmed the police view that not only had Ted practised witchcraft, but had taken the Left Hand, or black magic, Path. Both white and black witchcraft are largely based on psychic power – usually the full psychic power of a coven – with black magic merely being an inversion, an evil inversion, of white witchcraft. In a primitive form, a football crowd willing on the home team to win, is an example of the 'powers' that witches hope to exploit. The powers, practices and aims of witchcraft are quite complex and Wicca, as it is called, has its own theology – although not possessing a central fount of wisdom and authority as Rome is for Christianity, the practices and beliefs of different covens tend to vary considerably. Common to all, however, are the two deity personifications of witchcraft – the Horned God (the 'Devil' of Christianity) and the Mother Goddess – it will not have escaped notice that Ted often referred to me as 'Goddess Joan'. In his book, *What Witches Do*, the author Steward Farrar writes: 'Black magicians do exist, and although they run the daily risk of coming up against a stronger defence and destroying themselves by the boomerang effect of their own power, they can do a lot of damage while they last. By the nature of things, they are self-destructive, because in attempting to scale a path which should be used for spiritual progression, they are attacking heights where the price for black working grows more astronomical with every step. . . . Fortunately, although the black magician can (literally) get away with murder undetected by his ordinary fellow citizens, white magicians have their own ways of smelling his rat.' I do not think any of the police involved in the case against my husband would consider himself a magician, even a white one. But what is striking about the practice of witchcraft, either black or white, is that witches work with elemental forces – their year is based on the nature festivals, their God and Goddess are nature deities and they invoke and banish power with the Pentagram of Eearth.

It is easy to perceive that Ted's pre-occupation with witchcraft and magic should either arise from or lead to his deep knowledge of nature. There were other signs had I been alert enough to recognize them – not that any growing awareness that he might practice witchcraft would have ever led me to suspect him of his crimes.

One morning, for example, as I was hanging out the clothes at the back of the house, I happened to look down and there, almost at my feet, was the most ugly plant I have ever seen. I couldn't help gasping with astonishment and revulsion. It had a tall stem like a thick finger, shaped like a snake and it had a big red mouth and a black tongue. 'Ugh'! I shuddered and Ted, who had come along to see how I reacted, said, 'I was waiting for you to do that – I thought it would intrigue you'. He thought it was all very funny.

I usually looked after the garden and Ted usually brought me the plants. This had been buried in the soil, just in the corner where the steps lead up to our lawn.

'It doesn't intrigue me at all!' I said. 'Did you put it there?'

'Yes – I got it from old Berger's place. It was an old bulb I found. It's called the Devil's Lily'. Its proper name, in fact, is the dragon arum lily, and some people have mistaken it for the mandrake which is supposed to eat insects and which, it is also said, when plucked shrieks like a human being.

When the lily faded I decided to get rid of it. I trampled it underfoot and then flung rubble and stones over it certain that would kill it. Strangely enough, early in 1972 after Ted's conviction, I went out to feed the children's guinea pigs – and there was the lily again, this time with *five* stems instead of one I am not normally superstitious, but the very moment I caught sight of that lily, I slipped and fell over on the steps, wrenching my shoulder.

One other strange thing: a few years ago, Ted brought home a little blackbird. It was a baby and he said he had picked it up after it had fallen out of its nest. At first I thought it was a rook, but it grew and grew until I realized that it was a raven. Ted used to keep it in a cage in his workshop and attached a chain to it, so that he could walk around with it perched on his shoulder. We called it Caw – because of the sound it made; you'd hear it 'caw-cawing' all through the night. Ted eventually built a little house for it with a swing and a window. It became a great pet and we gave it all our left-overs. 'Send that to Caw' I used to say when I was clearing bits off the plates after a meal.

The odd thing is that following Ted's arrest, Caw vanished. I don't know how he got loose and I've no idea where he went to; but he disappeared. I was laid up in plaster for a few days while I was recovering from the fall 'due' to the lily. During this time my daughter came to me and said 'Mummy, Caw is back!' There on the lawn was the raven hopping about.

Then, a few days later, another car shot over a yellow line, straight into mine. We all laughed of course; making a big joke about black magic working – the lily, the raven, the car and the 'accidents' to me! It is easy to scoff at black magic and I am not seriously superstitious but it was a strange coincidence. Since Ted's arrest and the evidence that he has dabbled in black magic, and while I was in great distress and still very vulnerable during interrogation, I and my family started to wear gold crosses, but since then I have recovered some of my sanity and we now wear them only because they are attractive and a symbol of good in the world.

So many things that I paid little or no attention to at the time now seem to have a sinister or evil aspect. Both the lily and the raven come into that category. Then there was the night in August, 1970 when I was awakened by the sound of heavy panting or breathing from outside. I listened for a brief second as the sounds passed under my window; then the night was shattered by the most fearsome squealings; they were really horrendous. I jumped out of bed and went over to the window. I raised it and looked out.

Down the garden we kept a big cage housing the children's pets – various guinea-pigs and a pet rabbit. I could hear this clawing noise at the wire but I could see nothing. I thought Ted must be fighting someone who wanted to steal the little animals or some wild animal like a fox. So I shouted, 'Ted, what are you doing? What's wrong? What are you up to?' There was no answer and the breathing and squealing continued. The breathing was exactly like the sound of breathing made by someone suffering from an epileptic fit. Then, as I hurriedly put on my dressing gown preparatory to running down the stairs, both the squealing and heavy breathing stopped. Nevertheless, I still went down the stairs and outside, accompanied by Timmy, my terrier. I went to the cage where the guinea pigs and the pet rabbit, Skippy, were kept – and then suddenly stopped, drawing in my breath sharply. I felt terrified. Timmy was equally frightened. He wouldn't budge and I could see that his hair, like mine, stood on end; he neither barked nor whimpered nor moved. I have never seen a dog behave like that before or since.

A big hole had been torn in the side of the cage and every single pet was dead. Following Ted's arrest, the police suggested to me that this could have been some part of a black magic rite, but at the time no such idea crossed my mind.

I naturally told Ted the following morning and he dismissed the incident as having been caused by some animal. He showed genuine concern at the children's distress. He claimed he had found some hair there – and that it seemed to be that of either a stoat or mongoose. The police later checked with the State experimental farm because Ted told me he had brought the hair there for analysis; there was no truth in his story and the farm added there were neither stoats nor mongooses in the island. I believe that later Ted showed me a cutting from the local evening newspaper saying that there were wild polecats loose on Jersey and that they had been killing chickens. I accepted Ted's explanation at the time and I still cannot accept that I had a black magic ritual underneath my bedroom window.

Obviously, I was too easily taken in by Ted, because although he was lacking real education, he was so very well-read and seemed to have such a wide-spread knowledge not only of academic matters but of the practicalities of life. I knew he had no attachment to any particular church, nor, so far as I knew, any particular religion. Yet I thought he had a deeply religious sense. I remember one day discussing a Sunday paper supplement on space. 'You never know about space' said Ted, 'How do we know that there isn't another world behind space?'

'What do you mean?' I replied, puzzled.

'Well, a spiritual world. If our world can exist, then another world can exist. It goes on *ad infinitum* – there must be something behind it.' And for the next half-hour or so, he discussed this question of a spiritual world. It was impossible to listen to a man talk with such deep conviction about good and at the same time credit that he could be capable of the intense evil Ted wrought.

In his letters from prison, Ted reveals some of the curious workings of his mind and his far-reaching interests. He inevitably sign off his letters with the salutation, 'God go with you', or 'God willing', rather than the usual 'Yours sincerely' or something like that, and denies that he is a 'Satanist'. He considers the plight of North-east Ireland, following his reading of a poem by a young teenage Belfast girl and wonders how Christ would be treated in that city – probably shot in the back or told to mind his own business. He comments wryly that although Gurdjieff tells us that only conscious mental suffering is of value, bodily suffering does not seem to do one any good, either. He reflects on his first visit to the home and how hard my mother and I had it, washing nappies and all the rest of it – 'I have recived (received) so much happnes (happiness) through the home, I belive (believe) that we should have stayed there for it seem that I am only happy when I am helping people at least children I love to have big piles of kids around grown up annoy me but children never.' It spoiled his day to see that Gladys Cooper was dead. In a letter to his daughter Terrine, he says jokingly, 'I have of course though (thought) of flying across to Llanelly on my Broomstick only one of the screws (warders) as threaten to shoot my tail off anyway I believe the Welch warlock

137

are not very keen on we half French boys.' He sometimes wonders what he has done to 'get myself in this mess' still 'we are not the one who know the reason why'. If anybody wants to understand his way of thinking, they should read Ouspensky or Gurdjieff. 'Take the understanding of the East and the knowledge of the West and then seek. There is only one kind of magic and this is doing. Just try to find something more in life than just being.' He writes a long poem for Florence. His sorry to hear his Mum ('My Dear old Mum') is not in the pink and ponders that 'it must be that fellow Lang (Detective Colin Lang) putting a spell on you for being nasty to him'. He wants a check kept on Florence because she might find another chap and then where would he be – having to start all over again looking for someone else. He points out that 'Satians Templis' are allowed in England with the same rights as the C. of E. or the R.C.C. He repeats he is no Satanist but would fight for their right to worship the Devil if they so wished. He had been provided with the ammunition to fight his case 'not only the Balls but a bloody great cannon to fire it from' and speculated how he has changed, 'I us (used) to be sutch (such) a peacefull (peaceful) typ (type) now I am fighting mad.' He mentions how he built the home (Maison du Soleil) for me and the kids and not for himself, and how he has promised it to the children and me, during my life. He talks about having a long talk with the prison chaplain and discovering that he is a quiet being'. He adds, 'We had a chat about the way my group of friends look at God that we take the understanding of the East and the knowledge of the West and seek to find the truth'. Regrettably, the chaplain would not shift from his dogma that Christ was the 'begin and the end' – 'still we must try and understand there (their) way of think'. He was very optimistic that the 'Bobby (police) had done another Alphon De G' and that it might not be long before he was home again, the only trouble 'will be to get used to having to run thing again it as been so peacefull down here nobody naging at me'.

Poor Ted!

The police, in their various interviews in prison with him found his mind leaping about from one deep issue to another – on one occasion being concerned with Vietnam, the next Communism, the next the Common Market, the next, fishing. A curious philosopher *manqué*.

Gary Truscott lived in Vallée des Vaux and each Monday,

Wednesday, Friday and Sunday evening he usually either cycled or walked into Town to visit a youth club. On one such evening, in June 1970 he was walking home at 11.15 p.m., when he heard the sound of someone trotting or running behind him. He turned round to see a man in a dark track suit approaching. As the man came up with him, young Mr Truscott said, 'Good evening.' He got a mumbled sound in reply, which he took to be 'good evening.' The man went ahead of him, but later Mr Truscott saw him leaning against the hedge of a house. In the light from the car park of a nearby pub, he could clearly see that the man had a moustache and that his track suit was blue. One night in July 1970, he was again coming home from his youth club, this time cycling, when he saw the same man clinging to a tree from which it was possible to observe the same house.

At about 12.45 a.m. on 9th August 1970, the occupier of this house and his wife went to bed. Everything was silent and the door of the room where their two sons slept was open as usual. Sometime later, their 13-year-old son was wakened by a torch shining on his face. At first he thought the man holding it was his father but realized it wasn't when the intruder asked him 'where the money was kept'?

'I think I told him it was in the cupboard in the kitchen. He told me to get out of bed and asked me if I had a pair of slippers. I was frightened' said the boy in his court evidence.

Ted then told the boy that he would have to go out with him. When the boy asked why, Ted answered, 'there are two other people outside and they'll harm your father and mother if you don't go'.

Warning the boy to be quiet, Ted led the lad out by the window through which he had entered by releasing a catch and then brought him through a field to the back of the house. In the field, Ted asked the boy if his father was 'a bank clerk'? He then laid his raincoat on the ground (which the boy identified as being similar to one found in Ted's secret room). 'He then asked me to take off my pyjamas' said the boy, adding that he had done so. 'I think he (Ted) pulled his trousers down'. Before they left the field, Ted said he had lost his cigarettes and began looking around for them and then picked his cigarette lighter up from the ground. Ted then took him back to the house and he got back into his bedroom through the open window. He then removed his pyjamas trousers because they were wet.

The boy identified his attacker as 'fairly short with black

bushy hair' (hair which he identified as similar to the wig taken from Ted). Ted had worn a stocking mask over his face and had given off the smell of after-shave lotion – similar to the stuff produced in court.

The first the parents of the boy knew about the attack was when the lad entered their bedroom at 8 a.m., looking 'somewhat distressed' and inquiring 'if the house is all right?' He then explained that 'terrible things had happened to him during the night'. The father, leaving the lad with his mother, who discovered that he had been sexually assaulted, checked that the house was all right and on searching round the exterior of the house, discovered a brown glove which Ted had cunningly planted in the drive as yet another false clue. Dr Brian Hick, the lad's family doctor, examined the boy shortly afterwards. There were long scratches on the boy's face, extending almost to the crown of his head. He thought they must have been caused by brambles or fingernails. The problem was that there were no brambles near the house or the field where the boy had been assaulted and the scratches were so close together and so regularly paralleled that it did not seem they could have been caused by fingernails. When shown Ted's wristbands and his raincoat with nails, Dr Hick later formed the opinion that one or other of these were probably the real cause.

So far as the actual assault on the boy was concerned, the doctor believed that an unnatural act had been attempted, but the full act had not been completed.

One way or another, however, Ted Paisnel, the Beast of Jersey, had had his last fling.

Timmy, my terrier, was a very aggressive dog and he had a habit of tearing down the drive and barking at the dog next door which was a smooth-haired terrier. The morning of the day Ted was arrested, I had taken the muzzle off Timmy temporarily – I had been forced to put this on because Ted's sister had complained to Centenier Le Brun so often that I had no alternative – and, as is the way in these cases, Timmy had got out the door when I wasn't looking. As soon as he was out, he was off down the drive again and into a battle with next door's dog, Patchie. As a result they made more complaints to the centenier. When Ted came home for lunch that day, I told him about the row and said I had decided that Timmy would have to be put down – I didn't want any more rows about him. At three o'clock that afternoon, I went down into Town and had Timmy put to sleep. While I was away, I learned later, the centenier came up to see Ted – apparently Ted had had a frightful row with his sister and had struck her.

All that afternoon and early evening, I know, he stayed in his office. Later in his statement on arrest he said that he was so upset at the dressing down he had from the centenier that he sat down at his desk and started to drink beer. Then he took some tranquilizers and finally some painkillers that the doctor had recommended to him for his bad back. He sat there, growing more and more depressed, he said, until 9 p.m. – upset by the death of the dog and the centenier's lecture. Then he left the house and went off into the night. It was while he was in this state – loaded up with beer, tranquillizers and painkillers – he said, that in a daze he took the wrong car and having shot through a set of traffic lights, suddenly found himself being chased by the police.

When the police caught my husband, they had no less than twenty-one sexual attacks 'on their books,' as the jargon goes, extending right back to the late 1950s. To the police a common thread ran through them all and, initially, it was their hope that they would be able to charge him with them all. In the end, apart from motoring offences, my husband was to be found guilty on thirteen charges connected with six of the cases only. In the case of the alleged attack on the air hostess, Joy Mellish, evidence concerning the charge was heard in public in the lower court only, but the charge was not proceeded with – although not dropped – at the Royal Court hearing. When all twenty-one cases were first read out to him shortly after his arrest, Ted gave answers to some but maintained a non-committal silence about others; on one occasion, he gave the cryptic answer, 'That wasn't me – that was my shell' which left the slightly bemused police even more bewildered.

The police themselves now admit that even with my husband securely locked in a cell, the case against him was not an easy one to put together. In July Detectives Marsh and Lang, who were involved in the investigations under the overall direction of Mr Axon, the Chief Officer and the Detective Inspector George Shutler, felt that Ted Paisnel might get away with it – except for the motoring offences. It was in this mood that they decided to go back once more to the spot from which everything connected with the case had started – Vallée des Vaux and Grands Vaux – where Ted had lived for a while during the war; where he had

141

worked with the Germans; where the red scooter or motor-bike had been stolen; where a car had been stolen; where the last case of sexual attack had occurred. And suddenly their luck turned. They heard about Mr and Mrs Boston who not only were able to link Ted with the theft of Brigadier Starling's Rover and therefore, the alleged attack on Miss Mellish, but about Mr Truscott, a friend of the Bostons, who was able to identify Ted as the man he had seen hanging about the last house to be attacked.

Interviews, conducted by Mr Shutler, continued in the New Gate prison. Armed with these new facts and the various additional medical and forensic information that had become available, Ted was again questioned by the police on 27th August. By this time he had picked up some of the police jargon and talked about 'clearing the books'. He then told Mr Shutler, 'You do not have to call all the witnesses in the case. Write them all out and I will take them all.' Mr Shutler told him that this was not possible; they would have to go right through the list, one by one, and he would either have to admit or deny each case in turn. On a second occasion, again under questioning, he said 'I will take them all since the war – you write them down and I will sign it' and again, 'I told you I will take them all since the Occupation – now it is up to you'. The police still demurred at this approach but as they began to appreciate the difficulty of securing a conviction in all twenty-one cases, they once again made an approach, trying to secure a statement that would stand up in court. In the meantime, however, Ted's Advocate had advised him to make no statement confessing guilt either in a general or particular sense. When once again asked for his co-operation, Ted's answer has a curt, 'You've had your chance.'

The more the police delved into the case, the more weird it began to appear to them. Detective Inspector Shutler admitted to a reporter that Ted had apparently put a curse on him: 'Paisnel has told me that I shall be the subject of a spell and die of a heart attack before Christmas.' His doctor, however, had told him that he was 'good until I'm 90 – but strange things have happened in witchcraft and I'll be careful how I go in the next few weeks.'

Detectives Marsh and Lang repeatedly queried Ted about his beliefs – particularly about witchcraft. He neither admitted nor denied that he was a witch, parrying their questions with the remark, 'Why should you worry about something that hasn't happened to you yet ?' When they were questioning him as to why he painted everything he owned blue, at first he would not talk until they got him on to the subject of astrology and when he found that both Marsh and Lang were Gemini, he at once christened them 'The Gemini Twins'. At one stage, he implied that he would put a spell on them 'if they went too far'. At once Detective Lang shot out, 'You can't touch us – for the stone for Gemini is quicksilver and quicksilver is the natural antidote to witchcraft' – which, as Detective Marsh puts it, 'made me feel a lot better.'

Ted's reputation as a witch led to one curious incident in prison. Apparently, he developed the habit, possibly out of boredom, of drumming on the walls of his cell. He would start slowly, then work up into a tremendous steady rhythm of drumming. This annoyed one of the prisoners in the next cell who not only yelled at Ted to stop but began to joke about Ted's alleged powers as a witch. Whether to frighten the man or not, Ted 'put a spell' on him, telling him that he would 'drown in his own snot'. To the terror of the 'victim', he awoke during the night to find himself choking and unable to breathe. He was actually suffering from bronchitis and a large quantity of mucuous had built up during his sleep. The man flew into a panic and continued screaming until the authorities finally found a way of quietening him.

It was during one of the various interviews conducted by the police with Ted between his arrest and his eventual appearance in court that – Detective Sergeant Lang told the Royal Court – Ted raised the subject of his 'link' with Gilles de Rais. Ted explained that he 'traced his family back to 1300' and that he had been to France in connection with a search into his ancestry and claimed that his family came from a French town. 'He was very proud of his family history' Sergeant Lang told the court, adding that Ted had said in the book, *The Black Baron*, there was mention of the betrothal of a Joan Paisnel to Gilles de Rais in about 1400.

Let us, therefore, consider what other terrible influences may have been at work in helping to warp my husband's mind; in particular the black shadow of one of the greatest of history's monsters – Gilles de Rais, the original Bluebeard. Lest such an idea should seem fanciful, it may be worth recalling that both of Ted Paisnel's wives – and can anyone really doubt that it is mere coincidence – were called Joan Paisnel.

143

TEN

THE BLUEBEARD LINK

La Hougue Bie is a great mound, 267 feet above sea level, standing in the parish of Grouville in the south-east of the main plateau of the island. It is just under three miles from St Helier. It consists of a passage thirty-three feet long roofed with stones, leading to a Great Chamber, the whole covered by an immense mound of earth and rubble over forty feet high.

The word 'Hougue' derives from the old Viking word *Haugr*; meaning an 'eminence' and the Bie is thought to be a corruption of Hambye, for the lords of Hambye in Normandy owned this part of the island. By medieval times, the name had probably become La Hougue Hambye. The great stone tombs themselves, however, date from the days, probably around 3,000 B.C. when a people known to history as the Iberians (as late as the 5th century A.D., for example, the lower strata of Irish society were known as *Iberio*) began a steady progress across north-west France, thence into the Channel Islands and finally the British Isles where they have left similar impressive tombs, particularly near the river Boyne in Ireland.

Our concern, however, is not so much with the stone tombs themselves as with one of the small chapels on top of the mound and with the strange medieval legend and the history that attaches to it.

According to the legend, a dragon once lived in the marsh of St Lawrence in Jersey and created great havoc and dismay among the people of Jersey. In those days it was common to ascribe to pagan chiefs the attributes of a dragon – so we can read the legend more realistically as relating to a pagan chief or outlaw – or more probably a guerilla leader of the older race who carried on a resistance movement against the invading Normans. Anyway, according to the story, the Lord of Hambye, in Normandy, came to Jersey and defeating the monster, cut off its head. His attendant servant, however, was a treacherous rogue who in turn slew his master, then returned to Hambye declaring to the Lady of the manor that the dragon had killed her lord but that he, the servant, had killed the dragon in revenge. The last wish of his master, he then told the apparently gullible Lady, was that she should marry him. The Lady of Hambye accepted this explanation and became his wife. But one night, while asleep, the rogue shouted aloud his treachery and was subsequently brought to trial and his crime exposed. Then, on the ground where her slain Lord had been buried, the Lady of Hambye caused a mound to be built and on its summit a small chapel where masses were said for his soul. Mound and chapel could be seen from her castle above the village of Hambye in Normandy, a few miles from Coutances.

None of this would have anything more than an academic interest for us if it were not for the fact that my husband, Ted Paisnel, spent a lot of his time in this small chapel studying the coat-of-arms inscribed there and dreaming of the past glories of his ancestors – or those whom he liked to think were his ancestors. Hambye, in fact, *was* the seat of the once powerful clan of the Paisnels and it is true, for example, that Raoul Paisnel, Seigneur of Hambye, accompanied William the Conqueror to England. One of this man's descendants, William Paisnel, founded the Abbey of Hambye in 1145, the ruins of which can still be seen today in the valley in which the village lies. The Paisnels undoubtedly held extensive lands both in Normandy and England, where the name is spelt in a variety of ways – Paynel, Peynell, Paganell and so on. At the beginning of the 13th century, a grandson of the founder of Hambye Abbey, Thomas Paisnel, became Seignuer of Mélèsches in Jersey. This same man was granted the fief du Hommet in St Clement in 1208 by King John of England. Five years later, when the King of France seized the duchy of Normandy, the Norman knights who held lands in both France and England were ordered to make a decision as to their allegiance. Thomas Paisnel, who owned vaster estates in Normandy than he did anywhere else, chose to give his allegiance to King Philip Augustus of France and his estates in Jersey were therefore confiscated by the English Crown. There is no way of knowing whether the name lingered on in Jersey (it was usual for workers or retainers to identify themselves by adopting the surname of their lords) or whether some junior branch of the family returned to Jersey sometime about 1300. What is certain is that at the beginning of the 15th century, the line of aristocratic

Paisnels (or Paynels as the name was alternatively spelt) came to an abrupt end. And with it we reach the tenuous family link with that other and greater monster, Gilles de Rais.

Gilles de Rais was born in 1404 and by inheritance became one of the richest men in France. His father Guy de Laval and his mother Marie de Craon were distantly related and in order to inherit the rich Rais lands, which encircled the duchy of Brittany, de Laval dropped his own name and took that of de Rais. Gilles himself was born in the rather ominously-named Black Tower at the castle of Champtocé.

Neither his mother nor his father consciously neglected him; indeed, as the heir to a vast patrimony, they somewhat doted on him; nonetheless, seigneurial and social duties occupied much of their time and the boy saw all too little of his parents. He led a pampered and privileged existence, however, his slightest whim indulged in by a small army of hangers-on and servitors. In 1415, a grave misfortune befell him, one which many historians regard as a turning point in his mental and emotional development; he lost both his parents. There is some argument as to whether or not his mother died before her husband; indeed, whether she died at all. Some authorities insist she remarried – but if she did, she never contacted Gilles again which would indicate an extremely callous character; the probability, it is felt, in view of the complete disappearance of her name from history thereafter is that her death preceded that of her husband's. The latter died slowly after being gored by a wild boar.

Gilles was an extremely talented and able youngster, superb in everything he attempted. Following his parents' deaths, he was to fall under the influence of his maternal grandfather, Jean de Craon, a great lord of the most lawless type, dedicated to acquiring money by even the most unscupulous means. Jean's own son and heir fell at the battle of Agincourt and Gilles, already master of vast estates, thus became heir also to his grandfather's great fortune and lands. The young Gilles, bereft suddenly of his parents; then placed under the care of guardians and tutors, now abruptly found himself – all within a matter of a few months – under the legal guardianship of the grasping, greedy, shrewd and devious Jean. By every account, this succession of swift events, ending particularly in the guardianship of his grandfather, was the worst possible thing that could have happened to the young Gilles.

Jean at once tried to inculcate into Gilles some knowledge of political affairs and particularly his own acquisitive habits. He failed in both objects; Gilles remained a ninny so far as political ideas were concerned and instead of adopting his grandfather's habits of theft and exploitation, began to display extravagant tastes which were eventually to reach squandermania. While he was still only twelve-year-old, however, his grandfather started the search for a suitable bride for him; one, above all, with *money*. He eventually found her; her name was Jeanne (or Joan) Páynel, then less than four years old. When the greedy old man marked her down, however, the only thing that mattered was that she was one of the richest heiresses in all France, owning the lands of Bricquebec, Hambye and Gacé. That and the helpful fact that her father, Foulques, was dead.

According to the custom in the case of an orphan, Jeanne became a ward of the Crown of France until she had reached her majority. In order to protect her, the King placed her under the care of the Roche-Guyon family who, almost at once, decided to engage her to their own son, then only seven. When Jeanne's family protested, the Crown removed the girl from the Roche-Guyons and cast about for more suitable guardians. This was the moment for which Jean de Craon had been waiting. He persuaded Jeanne's grandfather, the Baron de Chateaubriant, to apply for custody of the girl, promising him a large sum. Without waiting for the judgment of the court, Chateaubriant and de Craon signed a marriage contract, betrothing her to Gilles. The court, however, frowned on this shoddy mano- euvre and placed her in charge of her aunt, Jacqueline Paynel and forbade any further discussion of marriage until she came of age. In the end Joan married one Louis d'Estouteville before finally becoming a nun and dying as Abbess of Notre Dame de Lisieux.

So far as I am aware, Jeanne Paynel and Gilles de Rais never even met. The lands of Hambye passed to the house of Longue- ville and later to that of Matignon, and the Hambye Paynels, as a landed, aritocratic family anyhow, became extinct.

My husband Ted was unquestionably fascinated by the Baron de Rais and the parallels between the two men are such – despite the gulf of centuries, rank, and sheer evil – that we must, perforce, follow the young prince's progress.

The young knight cut his martial teeth in a protracted war between the family of Duke of Brittany and the rival Penthièvres which resulted in the triumph of the former and the further enrichment of Gilles and his grandfather. The young nobleman returned as a hero to his castle to resume his normal life – in other words the unbridled indulgence of every whim and fancy, accompanied, according to his later confession, by enormous meals and bouts of drunkenness. He was, by this time, well on his way to becoming the richest man in Europe. At his castle of Champtocé he was thus able to conduct himself like a minor prince and tyrant, sitting on a throne and fussed over by everyone. From time to time he and his grandfather forayed forth to engage in some bloody raid or sortie against their rivals. Whenever he grew tired of the usual court entertainments, the young prince avidly turned to literature. One of his favourite books was Suetonius' *The Twelve Caesars* – a chronicle of vices and extravagance almost without parallel. There was the history of the Emperor Tiberius, for example, who engaged young men and women to perform every sexual fantasy the mind could conceive; who at feasts loved to fill his guests to the brim with wine, then tie their genitals so that they could not urinate; there were the chronicles of the Emperors Caligula and Nero who spent money on a scale rarely matched before and certainly never matched since. It is reasonable to suppose that Gilles hatched out some of his own fantasies from what he read in much the same way as my husband Ted undoubtedly did his.

By the age of twenty-one, Gilles de Rais, by dint of his own and his grandfather's warlike acts, must have felt himself all-powerful; above the laws of either Church or King. Like Ted Paisnel, he could be a complete charmer when he felt like it; but brutal and cruel when the mood took him. Unlike Ted Paisnel, however, he was rich beyond the dreams of avarice, with a great inheritance stretching over Maine, Poitou, Anjou and Brittany.

The career of Gilles de Rais falls naturally into three parts. The first concerns his childhood and period of adolescence. The second, his participation in the Hundred Years War when he fought alongside St Joan of Arc. The third, when he embarked on his terrible career of frenzied vice and murder and turned to black magic as a way of replenishing the enormous riches he had squandered. By any standards, the life of Gilles de Rais, to say the least, is fascinating – if approached in a calm, objective way. If culled over by a slightly unhinged or unbalanced mind, it is likely to prove a lethal weapon leading inevitably to self-destruction.

In the year 1425, the French prepared to renew the Hundred Years War. Although often presented as a war between France and England, this was not really a nationalistic struggle in the same sense as Britain's wars with Germany this century. Men still thought in rough terms of a united Europe – Christendom. The struggle was between a French king striving to assert the power and authority of his Crown over his great feudal barons – in particular those barons who through their holdings in France ought to have been his loyal subjects but who, because they also held the Crown of England, were strong enough to keep up the struggle. When Henry V fought the battle of Agincourt, he was really a rebel (and a large part of his army was French anyway).

Such was the success of the 'English' faction, however, and the political intrigues and line-ups of the time, that by the Treaty of Troyes of 1420, Henry V forced the recognition of his own pretty spurious claims to the French Crown. He was declared the legal heir of King Charles VI of France and thenceforward England and France were to be known as the Double Kingdom. His great rival – and the man who was eventually crowned King Charles VII following the feats of St Joan – had, in fact, been disinherited by his father and his mother had declared him a bastard. But the death of Henry V in 1422 gave the Dauphin (as Charles was still called) his chance.

Gilles almost certainly fought on the French side when they attacked the English at St James-de-Beuvron and were routed. He appears to have learned a number of military lessons from this defeat and when he set forth for the campaigns of the spring and summer of 1427, he was thoroughly prepared. His retinue was the most magnificent of all the nobles; his troops were better paid than most; and he had more spies than most nobles employed – and again he paid them better. Castle after castle fell to Gilles and his allies and he distinguished himself in the assault on the castle at Lude where the famous English captain, Blackburn, was personally slain by the young hero.

Gilles turned up in triumph at the Dauphin's impoverished court at Bourges where his career was further advanced by his cousin, the Chamberlain – a position roughly equivalent to that of a modern Prime Minister in Britain. He had everything in his favour – he was personally popular, being handsome, witty and gay and able to splash about more money than the Dauphin himself. It seems likely that his obsession with children – his 'little angels' as he liked to call them – was already beginning for it was at this time that he took into his service a ten-year-old boy known as Poitou who was eventually to go to the stake with him.

The French cause languished because of squabbles at Court. Meantime the English faction had taken the offensive again and began making a sustained effort to achieve a decisive result. Their strategy was to take the town of Orléans, pushing across the Loire and flinging Charles the Dauphin from the last of his dominions. By October 1428, the siege of Orléans had begun. If France were to be saved, it seemed, only a miracle could do it.

The miracle, in fact, was provided. In the person of Jeanne (or Joan) of Arc. Her appearance at court was preceded by many omens and prophecies. Her claims were simple. She would raise the siege of Orléans and would ensure that the Dauphin was crowned King of France in the cathedral at Reims. Gilles de Rais appears to have been at court in the castle of Chinon when she made her dramatic entrance and picked out the Dauphin although he tried to trick her by hiding among his courtiers. It was his association with her, certainly, that was to lead him to a pinnacle of contemporary fame and glory and make him a Marshal of France. He was chosen to lead the French army that was to accompany the Maid to Orléans.

There is no question that Joan claimed to be the agent of supernatural powers in setting out what she intended to accomplish. She ordered two special holy banners made according to the instructions of her Voices and asked for the sword that would be found in the church of St Catherine de Fierbois. When she joined Gilles and the rest of the army at Blois, she laid down a set of rules that led later ages to call her Puritanical Joan – although she was merely implementing the ordinary teaching of the Catholic Church. She ordered that all camp followers – the prostitutes who normally accompanied all armies – should either marry or leave within twenty-four hours. She ordered that there was to be no swearing or blasphemy. In addition every soldier in the army was to attend Confession before setting off and lastly all food and supplies levied from the peasants were to be paid for. The army set out on their march preceded by a small band of clergy singing hymns. Gilles de Rais rode at the side of the Maid as this great crusade began.

At first, the military commanders, including Gilles, who accompanied Joan were prone to treat her as no more than an illiterate peasant possessing the simple qualities of a sacred talisman. Certainly, she had little military skill and her strategy and tactics could be summed up in the words, 'Up and at 'em!' – God would do the rest. A short while after she had entered the beleaguered city of Orléans (an act which the besieging English were unable to prevent) she toured the defences, observing the English fortifications outside only to be greeted by shouts from the blasphemous enemy of 'bitch', 'whore' and 'cow-girl' (English soldiers had already become known as 'Goddams' to the French because of their swearing). On the late afternoon of 4th May, the Maid had scarcely lain down for a quick nap then she suddenly awakened again and insisted that her Voices had told her to 'go out against the English'. Without any idea of where there might be fighting, she rushed out into the street and rode towards the Burgoyne Gate to find that some over-zealous citizens had decided on a sortie against the English off their own bat. She took command and pressed the sortie towards one of the English besieging fortifications at St Loup. It was a disastrous move, for the English commander sent another force to take Joan and her forces in the rear. Lookouts on the ramparts of Orléans, however, saw her plight, and rang the church bells. Gilles at once gathered his troops and made a rescue dash. Not only were the English put to flight, but Joan and Gilles together took St Loup – the first victorious blow of the campaign. From then on, Gilles supported Joan whole-heartedly even when her plans proved to be against all orthodox military thinking and advice. On 6th May, against advice, Joan crossed the river Loire to attack English positions on the south bank. She had only a small force and although the English at first retired, the Maid ran up against a very strong bastion, the sight of which made the French quail. They were about to turn away, despite her orders, when Gilles once more came to her rescue and crossed the river to her aid. His action swayed the other French commanders and in short order they routed the English.

On Saturday, 7th May, Joan decided to attack the key fortress of Les Tourelles, upon which all the forces and strategy of the English besiegers of Orléans turned. While attempting to scale the walls that morning, Joan was hit in the shoulder by an arrow. Gilles caught her as she fell from the ladder and helped to take off her white armour so that the wound could be attended to. Joan herself retired for a short while, presumably to pray. Soon afterwards she announced that as soon as one of her banners touched the walls of the fortress, it would fall to the French. When a shout went up, she cried, 'All is yours! Enter the fort!' and within a few minutes all resistance collapsed. Joan wept as the English forces, attempting to make their escape by a narrow bridge, were all drowned when the French set it on fire.

The following day, Sunday, 8th May, the English left their fortresses and drew up in battle order in front of Orléans. Joan, accompanied by Gilles and the others rode out from the beleaguered city and faced them. Joan's orders were that as it was Sunday, the French were not to attack, but fight back if the English advanced. For an hour the two armies stood looking at each other, then the superstitious English abruptly turned away and raised the siege.

Other French victories quickly followed and Gilles, now no longer in command of the armies but promoted Marshal of France, helped Joan gain victory of Patay where more than 2,500 English were slain and the famous Sir Joan Falstaff was forced to flee for his life. On Sunday, 17th, July, the Dauphin was at last crowned King of France in the cathedral at Reims and Gilles' promotion was officially confirmed.

Joan of Arc, it is said, wept for joy.

Gilles was to rescue Joan of Arc for a third time when she was wounded during the siege of Paris, dragging her to safety after she had been shot by an English crossbowman who yelled 'Whore!' as he loosed his arrow. Thereafter their paths diverged as a truce intervened and the French army was disbanded. Joan went on to be burned as a witch by the English while Gilles, it has been suggested, led an abortive attempt to rescue her once more – though most historians regard this as merely fanciful conjecture.

The evidence suggests, instead, that he spent most of his time in the subsequent months behaving like a rather superior highwayman and bandit, raiding local magnates and holding them to ransom and squandering large sums of money on lavish entertainment. He took the field once more when the English broke the truce and laid siege to Lagny. Gilles assaulted them with such vigour and skill, however that they were forced to retreat in disorder – his first major victory not overshadowed by the presence of Joan. But his thoughts had already begun to turn away from the pursuits that had brought him so much contemporary fame and honour. If he had been slain by an arrow during one of these fierce engagements, history would have seen the Sire de Rais in a very much different light. For he hung up his lance and armour only to turn to perversion and child murder on an unparalleled scale.

ELEVEN

END OF THE BLACK BARON

Gilles de Rais began his series of child murders in 1432, most of his victims being small children looking as much as possible as he had himself when he was a child. The first murders occurred at the castle of Champtocé, whose sinister walls still stand and then at Machecoul. Although only thirty four murders could be directly charged against him, it is believed that his victims numbered over three hundred. Forty bodies alone were recovered from the castle of Machecoul and another forty from Champtocé. In addition, he lived at various times in his other castles at Malemort, La Suze and Tiffauges.

In his confession, read at Gilles' trial before the Bishop of Nantes, and also at concurrent civil proceedings, the page Poitou described what usually happened once a boy or girl had been seized or procured and had been led to an upper room in the castle were Gilles, seemingly in the presence of his most intimate friends, practised his extraordinary pleasures. I need scarcely underline the parallels with my husband's actions. Poitou swore that he saw Gilles:

> In order to practice his debauches with said children, boys and girls, against the use of nature, first with licentious passion take his rod in his left or right hand, rub it so it became erect and sticking out, then place it between the thighs or legs of the said boys or girls, not bothering with the natural female receptacle, and rub his said rod or virile member on the belly of the said boys and girls with much gratification, heat and libidinous excitement, until he emitted his sperm on their stomachs.

At the civil trial, Poitou went into further details:

> after having had an orgasm on the stomach of the said children holding their legs between his, he had considerable pleasure in watching the heads of the children separated from the body. Sometimes he made an incision behind the neck to make them die slowly, at which he became greatly excited, and while they were bleeding to death he would sometimes masturbate on them

until they were dead, and sometimes he did this after they had died while their bodies were still warm. . . .

If any of the children gave more trouble than suited Gilles, he handled them as follows:

In order to stifle the cries of the children when he wished to have relations with them, he would first put a rope round their necks and hang them up three feet off the floor in a corner of the room, and just before they were dead he would cause them to be taken down, telling them they would not utter a word, and then he would excite his member, holding it in his hand, and afterwards have an emission on their stomach. When he had done this, he had their throats cut and their heads separated from their bodies. Sometimes he would ask, when they were dead, which of these children had the most beautiful head.

Under torture by the civil authorities, Gilles made a 'voluntary' confession. He admitted that he had enjoyed his vice, sometimes personally cutting off the head of the child with a dagger or knife, at other times beating the youngsters to death with a stick, then kissing voluptuously the dead bodies, gloating over those who had the loveliest heads and the most attractive limbs. His greatest pleasure was to sit across their stomachs and watch them slowly pass away.

One of his servants testified that Gilles took more pleasure in the murder of the said children, and in seeing their heads and limbs separated from their bodies, in seeing them die and their blood flow, than in having carnal knowledge of them.

Afterwards, both the bodies of the children and their clothes were burned in the open fireplace upon great logs of wood. The ashes were generally thrown into the castle cesspit or moat.

Even as Gilles indulged his wildest sexual fantasies behind the grim walls of his castles, he also embarked upon a bout of extravagance that had scarcely been seein Europe since the last of the most debauched Roman Emperors. He embellished his castles until their interiors shone like golden palaces; he kept his own private army, richly clad in the most expensive materials of the day. He was attended constantly by jugglers, singers and entertainers. He kept lavish open house – the tables always laid with food or drink so that anyone could stop at his castle and refresh themselves.

His greatest project was the foundation and upkeep of his

Chapel of the Holy Innocents. Here he indulged to the full his passion for music and ceremonial. The choir, of course, consisted of 'little angels' who sang like cherubim – and who, it would seem, were usually immune from his carnal approaches. He lavished enormous sums on this chapel, raising it to the dignity of a cathedral – without the Pope's permission. He had several great organs constructed – and even a few small portable organs so that he should never be without music. Ted Paisnel, it may well be, was striving to emulate this magnificence in his own small way, by building his witchcraft altar and installing that organ on which my daughter used to play so innocently.

By 1435, Gilles was beginning to run short of money. There is plenty of evidence that he not only poured out his riches as from an unending river, but that he was lavishly cheated and embezzled by his own staff and the merchants with whom he dealt. Unable to conceive of poverty, however, or credit that even his resources were exhaustible and, presumably, in the grip of a mania that had not got out of control, he began to sell off his lands and possessions. Debts continued to pile up and many of his most precious treasures were sold off at absurdly low sums. In 1435, his heirs obtained an order from King Charles VII forbidding further sales, but the decree was ignored in Brittany where both Duke Jean V and his Chancellor, Bishop Malestroit, were eager to acquire properties. Foiled in his open efforts to sell castles or lands, Gilles either pawned or sold other treasures. In a single year, while he stayed at Orleans where he staged an impressive theatrical performance, he spent over £1 million. It was at this stage that he turned to alchemy, seeking the philosopher's stone that would transmute base metals into gold.

As with many another criminal, Gilles began by merely dabbing. He borrowed a book on Alchemy from a knight he met in Angers and in a room there, before several of his followers, he attempted to invoke the Devil. Little success appears to have attended this effort and his next move was to hire a goldsmith who, handed a silver mark, promised to transmute it into gold. This proved no more successful, the man locking himself in a room and getting drunk.

Two men who helped Gilles find someone with a knowledge of alchemy were his cousin, Gilles de Sillé and a priest from the Chapel of the Holy Innocents called Blanchet who appears to have played an unwilling part. Several reputed practitioners were found, one of who helped de Rais sign a pact with the Devil, using blood from his little finger. Gilles appears to have been constantly terrified at what he was doing and on one occasion, when tempted inside a magic circle, straightaway began saying a prayer to the Blessed Virgin which resulted in the magician ordering him from the room.

None of the attempts appears to have yielded any results for the next we hear is of Blanchet unearthing a mountebank called Jean de la Rivière who put on a performance convincing enough to persuade Gilles to give him a large sum for certain things necessary for the invocations – but de la Riviere disappeared with the money and was never seen again. Undeterred by this setback, Gilles sent Blanchet into Italy where in Florence he met a clerk in minor orders called Francois Prelati.

On arrival at Tiffauges, Prelati soon got to work. He and Gilles spend whole nights together in a lower room of the castle, invoking the Devil with the words, 'Come then Satan.' The best Prelati was able to achieve was a sudden cold wind, despite magic signs, circles and characters. Later, Prelati discovered a book in the possession of a local alchemist and an even more determined attempt was made to invoke demons. According to Poitou, Prelati made a great circle in the hall of the castle of Tiffauges with the point of a sword. And he made crosses, signs and characters, like armorial bearings, in the four parts of the circle. Helpers were ordered to bring 'a great quantity of coal, incense, a magnetic stone, an earthen pot, torches, candlesticks, fire and other things.' Everything was carefully arranged in accordance with the book and a great fire lit in the pot containing coal. After other preparation, everyone except Prelati and Gilles withdrew, the latter placing themselves in the middle of the circle. Further characters were traced; magnetic powder, incense and aloes were placed on the coal fire from which a stinking smoke ensued. For two hours, the two men alternately sat, stood or knelt, adoring the demons and making sacrifices to them – demons who were said to have the power to 'reveal hidden treasure'. Prelati's invocations were as follows: 'I conjure you Barron, Satan, Beelzebub, Belial, in the name of the Father, the Son and the Holy Ghost, in the name of the Virgin Mary all the saints, to appear in person, to speak with us and do our will.' The only upshot of all this was that the noise as of a four-legged animal was heard on the roof leading to the skylight of a pond where fish were kept – historians have speculated that the mysterious four-legged animal was nothing more sinister than a cat. The experiments continued every night for five weeks without evoking success.

It has been popularly supposed that Gilles actually indulged in human sacrifice, as he grew more and more desperate. Indeed, charge No 15 against him read:

According to initial reports of public gossip, resulting in a secret inquiry by the Right Rev. Bishop of Nantes, in his Town and diocese, by the agents of the Deputy Inquisitor and by the Prosecutor of the ecclesiastical court, into the following charges, all crimes and offences governed by ecclesiastical law and according to the lamentable outcries, tears and wailings, denunciations coming from many persons of both sexes, crying out and complaining of the loss and death of children, the aforesaid Gilles de Rais, accused (and his accomplices) have taken innocent boys and girls, and inhumanly butchered, killed, dismembered, burned and otherwise tortured them, and the said Gilles accused, has immolated the bodies of the said innocents to devils, invoked an sacrificed to evil spirits and has foully commited the sin of sodomy against young boys and in other ways lusted against nature after young girls, spurning the natural way of copulation, while both the innocent boys and girls were alive or sometimes dead or even sometimes during their death throes.

Other charges included one that Gilles offered 'the hand, the eyes and the heart of one of these said children, with his blood in a glass vase, to the Demon Barron, in sign of his homage and tribute.'

What has to be emphasized, however, is that Gilles de Rais' attempts to invoke demons or the Devil were in no way the reason why he committed the sexual assaults on the children and then murdered them. Anymore, I suppose, than my husband Ted's sexual assaults on women and children were the direct result of his practice of black magic.

Gilles continued his attempts and it seems that Prelati, after insisting upon being left alone, managed to 'raise' the demon Barron some ten or twelve times. The gullible Gilles appears to have believed these stories but neither Prelati nor anyone else was able to produce real gold.

Long before the end, whispers of Gilles' behaviour had begun to leak out and Bishop Malestroit had begun his investigations. Although he was aware that his behaviour was being looked into, Gilles continued both with the murders and with the invocations. His financial position had grown too desperate to give up the search for the alchemist's stone. It seems that like my husband Ted, Gilles had periods when he struggled to overcome his vicious habits and reform his life. He attended church, made his Confession and received the Sacraments; talked about a pilgrimage to the Holy Land. But as though driven by the forces of goodness to commit the final act of folly, Gilles attemped to repossess a castle and church he had sold to the Duke of Brittany by breaking into the church during mass and taking the castle officials prisoner. This gave the Duke the chance to move against him, for Gilles had violated both church and feudal law and the Chancellor, Bishop Jean de Malestroit, published his findings into Gilles' murders and devil-worship on 19th July, 1440.

On 13th September 1440, the first of the trial sessions opened. In all, 110 witnesses were heard. Although one of Gilles' assistants swore that Poitou had taken the hand and heart of a child, which had been placed in a glass and covered with a cloth, and left it on the chimney piece of the room where Gilles and Prelati tried to invoke the Devil, no evidence was given that the child was specifically killed for this purpose. Indeed, attempts by one of the prosecutors to link the invocations with human sacrifice was rebutted vociferously by Gilles. Prelati, for his part, insisted that he had never proffered the limbs and blood of a child to Barron, although Gilles had provided him with them for that purpose. Gilles himself insisted that no one or nothing had taught him to commit the assaults and murders – 'that he did it in accordance with his own imagination and thought, following no man's counsel, but his own, solely for his pleasure and carnal delight and with no other end in view.'

On 22nd October, Gilles made a full confession before the whose assembly. He made a long and comprehensive statement explaining 'with great bitterness of heart and much shedding of tears, that he had offended against our Saviour by reason of the fact that he had been poorly controlled in his childhood when, without check, he had applied himself to everything that might give him pleasure and had taken delight in all illicit acts.' One of his friends, years later, explained that Gilles, from earliest childhood expected everyone to be obedient and submissive to him, never daring to contradict or go counter to him. Certain psychologists hold that sexual deviations are mainly the result of the persistence of childhood feelings of guilt and inferiority

159

and the guilt always implies rejection and non-acceptance. It scarcely seems likely that as he was never punished nor corrected for anything he did wrong as a child, he was left with feelings of guilt for which there was never any emotional discharge.

On 25th October, Gilles was condemned to death, having been found guilty of 'perfidious, heretical apostasy and the invocation of demons as well as the unnatural vice of sodomy with children.' He was then handed over to the secular authorities for punishment. The civil court also charged him with murder (a crime with which the church courts were not empowered to deal) and he was sentenced to death.

At 11 o'clock the following day, after he had been excommunicated and then readmitted to the Church because of his contrition, Gilles was first strangled and then his body thrown upon the flames. In view of his contrite attitude, however, the court decreed that it was permissible to take the body from the flames before it burst open and to give it Christian burial – which was done. With him died two of his assistants, including the young page, Poitou.

Thus died the monster – one of the greatest in history – whose life and acts, even to the placing of the rope round the necks of his intended victims and unnatural carnal intercourse, were paralleled, if to a much lesser degree, by my husband Ted Paisnel.

Who can doubt that the sinister influences of the Black Baron did not cast a shadow on the mind of this Jersey farmer and builder, obsessed as he was with the knowledge that Gilles had been once betrothed to a Paisnel?

TWELVE

VERDICT

On the morning of Monday, 29th November 1971 after a five-day trial, the Bailiff of Jersey, Sir Robert Le Masurier, began his 65 minute summing-up in the trial of my husband, Edward Louis Paisnel.

The previous Friday, the Attorney-General of Jersey, Mr P. L. Crill had summed up the case for the prosecution. He said the prosecution's case divided into three sections: firstly whether the offences were committed at all in the places alleged and with the victims alleged; secondly, he would consider the identity of the attacker presenting both general evidence and individual evidence; finally, he would deal with the defence that had been offered.

The defence, he suggested, had not challenged the names of the people attacked, the dates on which the attacks took place, the times at which they took place or the venues. He would therefore confine himself as to whether the acts alleged were committed. It was clear that there would have to be corroboration of the evidence given by the victims, of the nature of the offences and the identity of the assailant. The victims, he submitted, had given perfectly consistent explanations as to what took place and corroboration was afforded by the medical and forensic evidence. All the victims had shown varying signs of distress.

The medical evidence clearly showed that the alleged acts took place on these people and on the dates and at the places mentioned. There was no direct evidence, of course, linking the accused with these offences. The accused had not been seen during any assault or running away afterwards. The evidence, therefore, was circumstantial, but that was no derogation. Circumstantial or indirect evidence could be a mathematical proposition and a clear and unequivocal picture would emerge. The evidence was a jig-saw puzzle but he would produce relevant details to solve it. If the Court found that the complaints were consistent with what had happened to the victims, then the Court might find that the facts were consistent with the matter of identity.

First, Paisnel had 'borrowed' a car and driven through the red lights. But why should a man having committed these two offences drive like a fiend ? – the only reason he was caught was because he finally ran out of steam. Paisnel had risked his life in the chase, probably because he did not want the police to find what he had on him, and secondly because he did not want them to track down what he had at home.

His first lie was that he had a bad heart. There was no medical evidence concerning this. With regard to cigarettes, Paisnel, in fact, was a non-smoker yet in two cases he had given his victims reason to believe that he was a smoker, because in one case he had said that he had dropped his cigarette lighter while in another he had said that he was 'getting a packet of cigarettes'. These were deliberate attempts to lead a false trail for the police.

It had been shown by expert witnesses that the nails in the coat and wristbands were no deterrent against karate or judo (as Ted had claimed). And there was no evidence that Paisnel had been threatened or needed protection – apart from the case of the French worker many years ago (when Ted was hit over the head with a potato box).

Dealing with the articles in the hidden room, Mr Crill referred to the tracksuit which had mud on the elbows. This mud, he submitted, could have come if someone were being assaulted on the ground. How also did Paisnel know that the police were referring to nails in the coat when they told him during the interviews, that blood had been found – unless he knew that this coat had come into contact with someone who had been scratched ?

Paisnel had explained the seminal stains found on his raincoat as having been caused either by his dog or when he himself had had intercourse on it. Miss Hawkins, who had been the accused's mistress for at least the previous two years had said she knew of no other women who had had an association with Paisnel during that time and had said in evidence that she had never seen the raincoat. Also the Official Analyst considered it highly unlikely that a dog could have caused the seminal stains because of their position and size.

He believed that the hidden room and its contents must be

puzzling the Court. So far as these were concerned, no defence witness had ever seen any of the strange items of clothing. If their connotation were an innocent one, why had they not been seen? Only Miss Hawkins appeared to know of the existence of the hidden room and she had only seen it in the dark. 'It was an ideal place for hiding clothes which this man was using in the series of attacks on these victims. It was well hidden and it was kept locked with a barrel lock which was practically impossible to find.' The Official Analyst had given evidence that all the clothing examined had had a musty smell and if this clothing was put to normal use, there was no reason why it should have this smell. Why also was Miss Hawkins so agitated when she found the police examining the cupboard? – he suggested that the reason was that she knew more than she had told the Court.

Paisnel's explanations to the police in answer to their questions were neither consistent nor supportable. Four days after his arrest he had complained that on the night of his arrest he was confused and upset, but there was 'not a shred of evidence to support this'. When told that his description fitted that given by several of the children, he had said, 'Well, they are not little kids now.'

'How did he know their ages?' asked Mr Crill. 'I suggest it was not just from reading the *Evening Post* [the local Jersey newspaper]'.

Mr Crill then referred to Ted's remarks 'which the Court might consider a general admission of the offences'. These referred to the occasions on 16th July and again on 27th August when he had said he would 'clear the books'.

'If that was not a general admission, I do not know what was,' said Mr Crill.

The Attorney-General then went on to deal with each of the assault cases. In the case of the most recent attack, on the 11-year-old boy in Vallée des Vaux, Mr Crill said that while the boy had the same blood grouping as the accused, he was too young to have produced semen. The scratch marks on his face were obviously from the wristbands or coat; there was no bracken or brambles in the field which could have caused these marks. The boy had also identified the after-shave lotion. Several witnesses had testified that Paisnel knew Vallée des Vaux well – and there was no doubt that it was he who had fallen on to the roof of Bostons' house. He had been also seen wearing a blue tracksuit shortly before the attack and had been

163

seen on three other occasions in the area. The boy had identified a 'musty' smell from his attacker's clothes.

In the case of the girl who had been attacked at Trinity in 1966, the girl's blood group was different to Paisnel's The scratch markings on her back were consistent with the attacker wearing wristbands and grabbing her round the waist – again there was neither bracken nor brambles to cause the damage. The girl had been given every chance to hear the man's voice and was quite sure it matched the tape recordings of Paisnel's voice played in court. Paisnel also knew the Trinity area well, having gone to school there.

So far as the letter received by the police threatening to commit the perfect crime was concerned, Mr Crill submitted that there were far more similarities with Paisnel's usual writing than dissimilarities – besides my daughter had identified his writing without even being asked.

In the third case, in which a girl of ten had been attacked at St Martin, a pubic hair had been found on a rug and evidence clearly showed it was identical to that of one of the accused's, especially as regards to colour. On that occasion, the attacker had worn a type of yachting cap, similar to that found at Paisnel's home. The attacker had also talked to the girl about the Navy.

In the case of the boy attacked at Grouville, another pubic hair had been found identical to Paisnel's.

When a young girl had been attacked at St Martin in 1960, she had given evidence that her assailant had worn a duffle coat. Later, a duffle coat found in Paisnel's home had been identified by a witness who said it matched the one stolen from his car three weeks before the attack on the girl. As regards the assailant's use of the word 'bejesus' – this was a word witnesses had said commonly used by the accused. Both mother and daughter had identified the voice they heard on the tape-recording in court as similar to Paisnel's.

Finally with regard to the boy who had been assaulted in a football changing hut at St Saviour, Mr Crill said that shoe impressions found at the scene were of a similar size to those worn by Paisnel. A piece of cotton wool found in Paisnel's bed-sitter was similar to one found at the scene of the attack. The photograph of the boy's house found in the loft over the hidden room had been taken, in fact, sometime between 1957 and 1960, although Paisnel said 'it came from the war'.

The sashcord found on Paisnel yielded a further inconsistency in his story. He had said he used it to work a concrete mixer in his yard. Why, when there was already a perfectly good one on the mixer?

So far as the secret room was concerned, the evidence showed that it had been built about 1968 and many of the offences had been committed before that time. However there was ample space at Maison Du Soleil to hide the incriminating clothes before the room was built.

Mr Crill then invited the Court to consider the facts in the first case and their similarity with the other offences. If the Court felt that Paisnel were concerned in the first case, then they could take into account the similarity with the others. There had been no denial in cross-examination that the offences had occurred – the case, therefore, was one of identification. He submitted that the list of similarities he handed to the court assisted in establishiug this identification – among them the wearing of a mask or scarf, threats to the victims, blood group-ings and the fact that the offences had occurred on Saturday or Sunday nights. As for the case for the defence, only two specific alibis had been produced. The first concerned Miss Hawkins – 'an unfortunate woman, a figure of some pity and who was obviously under Paisnel's thumb. She gave the impression of someone almost frightened.'

Miss Hawkins had told the police that Paisnel spent almost every Saturday night with her. Yet in evidence she said that Paisnel had stayed at her place only on a few occasions, and mostly on Saturday nights. Paisnel himself had said that he was with Miss Hawkins one night and he remembered it because he had had a parking ticket – but there was no evidence of this ticket. In considering Miss Hawkins' 'strange evidence' and the way she behaved when the police sought to enter the hidden room, her evidence was weak.

There was also an inconsistency in the evidence given by Paisnel's parents (who had sought to provide an alibi for him on the night of one of the attacks).

Advocate T. A. Dorey, defending my husband, and replying to the Attorney General said that the fact that the assailant had been wearing a cap or hat, a coat and carrying a torch were, in the circumstances of a man being out alone at night in the country, of small significance.

He suggested that Miss Hawkins became agitated with the

police because of the state in which she found the room as the police searched.

While there was no dispute as to the dates, times and venues of the assaults or the names of the victims, there was some dispute about the nature of some of the crimes committed. Of the three attacks on boys, two alleged sodomy and one alleged attempted sodomy. He considered the medical evidence could only support a charge of indecent assault in these cases.

He also took issue concerning the tracksuit which had been mentioned in the 1970 case. The tracksuit owned by Paisnel had not been identified by Mr Truscott who had said in evidence that the tracksuit he saw was of a lighter colour. Tracksuits were common. The evidence concerning a duffle coat was also unsatisfactory. One of the victims was doubtful whether her attacker had worn a dufflecoat or an overcoat – and anyway, ten years ago, dufflecoats were common. Wellington boots were also common. Mr Truscott's evidence was confused and unsatisfactory in that no proper identification parade had been held by the police.

Mr Dorey emphasized the voice differences as identified by witnesses in their descriptions of their assailant. One had said they had heard a husky voice with a Jersey accent, another had said that he had not spoken like a Jerseyman. A third had said the voice was very rough and did not have an accent, while someone else had said that the man sounded like a Jerseyman. Another opinion had been given that the voice was a high one and cultured, but rather like a working man's voice. There had been differences about the man's height.

He also queried the validity of the identification of a voice heard for a few minutes as much as eleven years before with a voice heard on a tape-recorder. He was not even sure how valid a voice heard on tape was – he believed the identifications would have been valid only if several voices had been played over on tape and the witnesses had been asked to identify the one that resembled that of their assailant.

The use of the word 'bejesus' was common to Irishmen and that there were many Irishmen in Jersey. As for the after-shave lotion, most of these after-shave lotions smelled the same. The cottonwool the police had found proved nothing – it could easily have come from a medicine bottle. He submitted that the assailant's talk about cigarettes was not a red-herring, as the prosecu-

166

tion alleged. Police evidence that the 'centre' of the assaults (a police 'map' of all the sex assaults and in particular those brought before the court was said to show Le Boulivot de Bas as the 'centre' from which these attacks had radiated – none was more than about $2\frac{1}{4}$ miles away) was Le Boulivot was wrong – it was Grands Vaux. As for the scratches on the two victims, medical evidence was that they might have been caused by fingernails.

'How the scratches were made has not been satisfactory resolved. But the case for the defence is that on those two occasions, Mr Paisnel has an alibi (one by his parent, the second by Miss Hawkins). If the Court decides that wristbands of this type were used, they must have been used by some person other than Mr Paisnel.'

So far as the secret room was concerned, it was not a secret room. It had not been built secretly and Miss Hawkins had seen it in 1969. It had the appearance of a rough storeroom used to give access to the loft. The door was behind the cupboard to avoid an unnecessary wastage of space. It would have been difficult to fit in the door and the cupboard without disposing of some other furniture. 'It was done purely on aesthetic grounds. There was nothing sinister about this door,' said Mr Dorey.

There was no evidence that Paisnel had ever worn the tracksuit discovered in the secret room. As for seminal stains on the raincoat, two possible explanations had been given. Miss Hawkins' statement that there had been no other women during the time she had been associating with Paisnel was, he was afraid, 'a belief in which a lot of women are often mistaken.'

He then dealt with the explanations given by the accused for his strange clothing. When first questioned, he had explained it by talking about 'his group of little friends'. It was only later that he had tried to rationalise his statements by talking about gadgets (Ted had argued that he used the wristbands and nails on his coat to assist with a builder's 'float' and also to assist with his roof-climbing in the legitimate course of his business). The Court had to ask itself whether there was a group of people to which Paisnel belonged who were devotees of 'some strange cult'. If there were such a group, 'they might well feel the need to wear some disguise whatever they met for, when they were out performing.' As regards his claim that he had worn the nails as 'protection', there had been a number of cases, particularly in England, where people who were different from others had been the victims of outsiders – Paisnel himself had been assaulted in 1965 by a 'Peeping Tom' (the fight in which Ted got hit with the potato box).

'The Court could also draw the inference that all this was fantasy and that Mr Paisnel was acting out this fantasy in a Walter Mitty life of his own. His wearing of strange clothing could be a slightly macabre extension of a schoolboy's love of dressing up. Some of the books which Mr Paisnel had might have encouraged the development of these fantasies. The accused's two offers of 'omnibus confessions' could be explained by his fantasies. His behaviour indicated some inbalance which might be the reason for various inconsistencies in his statement. He may have found it difficult to separate his real life from fantasy.' Mr Dorey concluded his case by insisting that the prosecution evidence was not strong enough. It was up to them to have proved conclusively that Paisnel alone carried out the offences and not that he *might* have done them.

On the following Monday, then, the Bailiff began his instruction of the two Jurats – Jurat F. E. Luce and Jurat A. A. H. Downer – as to how they should direct themselves in considering the evidence which they, in this case, would do in place of the usual jury.

The Jurats must not be influenced by the revolting details of the cases otherwise their emotions might take precedence over their dispassionate judgment.

All the offences, he reminded them, had been committed in the eastern part of the island and all concerned secluded houses. The *modus operandi* had involved prior observation of these secluded houses; the victims were young people or children. The offences constituted a particular type of depravity and in nearly all the cases there had been threats to the victims or their parents. Again, in nearly all the cases, a raincoat was worn by the assailant and a torch used. There were, however, dissimilarities. In one case, the assailant did not go to the bedroom but was seen by a mother in the kitchen and in a second case, the assailant was waiting in a drive for the young girl to arrive. Four of the cases had occurred on a Saturday or Sunday, one between Sunday and a Monday and another between Thursday and Friday. Nevertheless, all had occurred, it was suggested, at weekends. The Jurats had to be certain that the characteristics in each case were so common that the same man did them all. If the Jurats did not consider there were common characteristics, then they must consider each count in isolation.

Sir Robert said that none of the evidence could 'positively identify the assailant' but with one exception, none of it excluded the defendant. The accused had been in possession of all the articles of clothing mentioned by the various victims but, with the exception of the wig, they were common articles in common use. Evidence had been given by two of the victims that their assailant was a smoker, but there had also been clear evidence that Paisnel did not smoke. The prosecution invited the Jurats to find that the assailant mentioned cigarettes deliberately to mislead and the Jurats were 'entitled to ask themselves why empty cigarette packets were found in the accused's coat ?'

The Bailiff considered that the evidence given by Mr Truscott and Mr and Mrs Boston in connection with seeing Paisnel in Vallée des Vaux should be 'treated with some reserve' because this kind of identification was 'notoriously unreliable'. However, Mrs Boston had also claimed to have seen the accused under very unusual circumstances some months later.

He considered that little reliance could be placed on the identification of the assailant's voice with that heard on the tape-recorder in court 'because it could be very misleading'. And the anonymous letter 'could have been written by anybody with a distorted mind.'

So far as blood groups and pubic hairs were concerned, the Bailiff pointed out that in every case except one, where there was no evidence available as to the blood grouping the assailant was in, the assailant had always been in Group O. The Official Analyst had given an analysis of the likely percentage of the population that would fit into this category – but that analysis 'remained speculative'. However, it was of help to the Jurats as to whether more than one person had committed the offences because it indicated that the more limited the field, the less likely it was that more than one person fitted the evidence. As to the pubic hairs found on the scene of two assaults – they *could* have come from the accused because they were an identical match, but it had *not* been proven that they did come.

As to the scratches on two of the victims, two doctors had said that they could not have been caused by vegetation in the area but could have been caused by the nailed wristbands. Human blood had been detected on one of the bands but the owner had not been identified. It had not been possible to

169

determine whether the blood on the other wristband was human or animal.

With regard to the seminal stains on the raincoat, the accused had explained that he had had intercourse on the raincoat and so it had to be assumed that he was admitting some of the stains were his own. Although Miss Hawkins had said she had never seen the raincoat before, this did not prove that the defendant had not had intercourse with some other woman and there was no evidence as to the age of the stains.

Regarding the arrest of the accused, the prosecution had alleged that he was on the way that night to inflict 'another nightmare on another victim'. The defendant's explanation of his behaviour, however, was that he was under the influence of an overdose of drugs after a row with his sister. Alternatively, the defence was that he had been on the way to a meeting of a group of people with an unusual way of life. If this were true, said the Bailiff, the Jurats had to ask themselves why Paisnel had taken someone else's car? Although he had offered to accept responsibility for all sex crimes of the nature of which he stood accused since the Occupation, he had never said anything that amounted to an admission of any particular offence. As to the photograph of the house of one of the victims, he had given three explanations for possessing this: firstly, that the photograph had been taken during the war; secondly, that he had bought it at an auction; thirdly, that it was in some books he had sold to the owner of the house. As to the two alibis – if the Jurats accepted these, then there could be no certainty that all the offences had been committed by one man.

My husband, Ted Paisnel was found guilty on all thirteen charges connected with attacks on six people, all but one of whom were minors. The outstanding charges concerned with his alleged assault on the air hostess, Miss Joy Mellish, who had given her evidence in public before a magistrate, were not included – although the two charges involved were not – and still have not been – dropped.

It took the two Jurats just thirty eight minutes to reach their verdicts. Ted was then remanded in custody for sentencing by the Full Court. In the meantime, a psychiatric report was to be prepared.

On Monday, 13th December 1971, before a Full Court with nine Jurats, my husband Ted, clad in fawn trousers, a blue

170

jumper and shoes still spotted with paint, showed no expression as the Attorney-General described him as a 'cunning, hideous man who appears to show no remorse, horror or emotion for the crimes he has perpetrated'.

The Attorney-General explained that there were two sets of indictments before the Court. The first concerned seven traffic offences, all of which had occurred the night Ted had been arrested. The second set concerned the sex offences of which he had been found guilty on 26th November. The Attorney-General, having read these out, said that the defence had asked for an electro-encephalogram examination. Before this was granted, he invited the Court to read the psychiatric reports which had been prepared by a London psychiatrist, Dr Nuestatter, and a Dr Evans. The Court proceeded to read these reports.

When the Court had finished reading, Mr Dorey, Ted's advocate, said that he wanted to draw the Court's attention to a point raised by Dr Evans as to Ted's mental condition. He said that a question raised in this report (neither report was nor has been made public) had not been answered. Dr Evans had said it was impossible to regard anyone guilty of such offences as normal. Although an electro-encelphalogram was not imperative, he thought it advisable in all the circumstances that such a test should be carried out before sentence was passed.

The Bailiff inquired as to the purpose of such a test. Mr Dorey's argument was that it would give some information on the question as to whether Ted should be considered sane or not.

'How could this assist the Court and what could the Court do?' queried the Bailiff.

Mr Dorey said that he thought it would affect the question of mitigation and would show to what extent the accused was governed by some uncontrollable impulse.

Elsewhere, perhaps, a Court might have been sympathetic to this idea. It has become fashionable to concern oneself more with the mind, attitude, condition and possibility of reforming a criminal than simply taking the more obvious, if less subtle, approach of putting him away as quickly as possible in a place where he can do no more harm. The Court of Jersey, which had firmly stamped on all attempts to introduce the black magic aspects of Ted's case into the court hearings and had insisted that all concerned should keep their feet firmly on the ground, leaving abstract speculation and theory to the sensational press or others, was in no mood to pursue the will o' the wisp of whether my husband was mentally unbalanced or not. Dr Nue-statter's report, which had been particularly requested by the defence, in the event, had proved more sympathetic to this view than towards the one Mr Dorey had hoped for. Although it was not mentioned in Court, the London psychiatrist had not con-sulted the police or their files on the case before examining Ted. His conclusion – which may or may not have been affected by any such consultations – was an unequivocal verdict that Ted 'was fit to plead'. Armed with this, a Court, representing the outraged burghers and citizens of Jersey who, to be absolutely fair, thirsted not so much for blood as for reassurance that Ted's reign of terror was over for good, took what many might con-sider a good old-fashioned view.

'We are not so much concerned with culpability,' announced the Bailiff. 'We are concerned with the community'.

Advocate Dorey made a last forlorn attempt to save his client from the full rigours of the law. His plea was trendy enough to satisfy the producers of the BBC's *Man Alive* programme: 'We must consider the accused as well.'

The Attorney General intervened to point out that the psychiatric reports that had been prepared, particularly that of Dr Nuestatter, had not given any indication that an electro-encephalogram was necessary.

The Full Court of Jersey, whatever its feelings might be as to the need to protect the community, was by no means prepared to ride roughshod over any of the accused's rights. Reports by probationers and psychiatrist were already in their hands; was a electro-encephalogram really necessary? They retired for fifteen minutes to debate the point among themselves. They then returned to announce that they could not see how such a test could assist the Court.

The Attorney-General then began a summary of the charges, so that the Court could decide on fit sentences. Paisnel, he said, had been unhelpful to the police, apart from his two efforts to make 'global' statements. The car chase, in police opinion, had been the worse they had ever had to face. Twelve of the sex charges involved young children; some the most revolting of their kind.

Over a long period, the people of Jersey had faced deep and grave anxiety. Parents had been distressed; others, as the result of police inquiries, had faced deep and distressing suspicion.

One girl had been nearly strangled; another had the same sort of treatment meted out to her.

Under customary law, said the Attorney-General, the penalty for rape was death – in the United Kingdom now that had been reduced to life imprisonment. The maximum penalty for sodomy was life imprisonment both in Jersey and the United Kingdom.

'I do not know the motive behind these assaults' said Mr Crill, the A-G., 'but although much has been written in the popular Press about black magic, this has never been part of the case for the defence'. He added, 'The suggestion that Paisnel had been acting out a fantasy had not been borne out by the psychiatric reports.

'This is a man who deliberately gratified his lust on young children as and when he wished. Paisnel had forfeited his right to freedom and liberty for a considerable period of time. Less than a hundred years ago he would have been in peril of his life. He is a cunning and hideous man, who appears to show no remorse, horror or emotion for the crimes he has perpetrated.'

Advocate Dorey insisted that in view of the psychiatric reports, 'it is not safe to formulate any conclusions'. He pointed out the absence in the sex cases of the gross brutality that was generally associated with sexual assaults on children. In these cases of rape and sodomy there was only minimal penetration and in spite of threats to kill victims or their parents, there was, in fact, no infliction of permanent injury. A second point in mitigation was Paisnel's excellent character, apart from the driving offences and one committed during the Occupation under the Germans (Ted had served a month's imprisonment). The Honorary Police had said he was a law-abiding and well-behaved person and this good character, he thought, ought to be taken into consideration by the Court. There was more chance of a successful rehabilitation than if he had been a brutal person. Another point in his favour was his kindness towards children which had been stressed in the reports before the Court. He had done good work at the children's home and in view of his kind behaviour towards children, all the offences seemed out of character. The question of motivation was therefore very difficult to answer.

The Attorney-General had demanded thirty years imprisonment; he thought fifteen would be more appropriate.

Following a thirty-minute adjournment to consider the sentences, the Court returned at 11.35 and confirmed the Attorney-General's demand for sentences totalling thirty years.

Ted had planned a new kitchen, new bathroom and a new roof for the part of Maison du Soleil in which I lived – just for me and the children. He was going to put a flat on the top floor and let it at 8 guineas a week in order to recover the money he would have to borrow from the bank to do it all.

I have been asked why I married Ted Paisnel? – was it for security? My answer is always the same – I was secure, in the financial sense certainly, before I married him. I had my work with the children and I could care for as many foster children as I wanted. Ted Paisnel was far from being rich – indeed, he had no money at all and the house and bit of land around it he bought after we were married from his parents for a nominal sum.

The immediate results of his arrest and sentence, however, were to leave me, as most non-working wives and mothers would find themselves, in straightened circumstances. He had an overdraft of some £1,000 and had some unpaid bills when arrested – and the bank immediately stopped further credit. I have had to take a small job which keeps me busy from 9 a.m. to 5.30 p.m. All the little luxuries of life have now gone, particularly in my small daughter's case – her riding lessons, piano lessons, dancing lessons, have all had to be stopped. Any monies coming in have to be spent on the essentials – food, light, heat. These difficulties apart my life in Jersey since the trial has been marked by the kindness and sympathy of the people of Jersey, among whom I hope to be able to continue to live.

The effects on Ted's family has been disastrous. A young lodger who came to stay with his parents discovered, I believe, that Ted was their son and one day my mother-in-law walked into the young man's room to find press cuttings of the case strewn all over the place and chalked on the wall the legend, 'What does it feel like to be the Mother of a Monster?' Only a short while ago, possibly due to the stresses set up by Ted's conviction, she died.

All of us have been upset by the large number of sightseers – many of them holiday makers from England – who in coaches and cars have paused outside Ted's office which still bears the large padlock placed there by the police.

I have been more concerned to protect my children – in particular, my small daughter. She believes her father has been put in jail simply because he drove a car too fast. Almost my first action was to send her away to a school to escape some of the gossip consequent on Ted's arrest. Up till recently, we managed to protect her from the real truth. But she had a fight with one of her schoolmates a short while ago. A little girl had shown her a trick but told her, 'Don't tell Jane'. My daughter forgot, however, and told Jane. So the other little girl said, 'You've told my secret, so I'll tell yours. My mummy says I mustn't – but I'm going to. Your Daddy's the monster – the Bogeyman!'

My daughter returned, her eyes red with weeping. She told me, 'Oh, mummy, I don't want to go to that school anymore – I don't even want to live in Jersey any more. Everybody now knows. Can't we go away some place.

I've toyed with the idea of emigrating to Australia and changing our names. I can foresee a future, if we continue to live in Jersey, where one day she may fall in love and the young man's parents will say, 'Don't you know who her father is?'

But I am now 51 and if I were to go to Australia I would have to satisfy the authorities that I was able to support my children and earn a living for them all. That, alas, is not as easy as it sounds. Nor would I have the money to buy a house, as under Jersey law a wife receives only a dower house and third of any money left.

Ted has said that he built the quarters where the children and I live at Maison du Soleil for us, not for himself (he wrote this in a letter to his mother), and that he hoped some arrangement could be reached so that the property could be leased or sold and the proceeds go to the support of myself and the children.

In spite of all the difficulties I do not feel that Ted has ruined *my* life. I am only sorry that he has ruined his own and affected the lives of others. Above all, I am sorry that he has cast a shadow over his daughter's life – a shadow which may disappear for a time but who knows when or where it may re-emerge and what tragedy it might spell for a child already, one would have thought, sufficiently afflicted.

On Wednesday, 6th September, 1972, the Channel Islands' Appeal Court heard Ted's appeal against both his conviction and sentence.

His Advocate, Mr Michael Clapham argued that the Bailiff had misdirected the two Jurats who tried the case in place of a jury. Mr John Godfrey Le Quesne, Q.C., who headed the

Appeal Court, giving the Judges' reasons for dismissing the appeal against conviction said that although it was true that the evidence of identification linking all the cases was 'entirely circumstantial', they were satisfied that he was the man who had attacked a 11-year-old boy in 1970 and raped a girl aged 15 in 1966. The Judges were satisfied that the Jurats were correct in deciding that the attacker in all the cases was the same man. As to sentence, this would stand at 30 years because the assaults on small children 'were horrifying and brutal in a very high degree'.

Ted created an enormous commotion in Court once the Judges had given their verdicts. He yelled out what he had been 'framed' and had to be dragged away to the custody room. As he was being hauled out of Court, he shouted: 'I was framed by the bloody lot of you – by Shutler and you' (meaning the Judges).

As he was dragged away, he passed the little group of police officers who had been responsible for his capture, arrest and conviction, among them Inspector Shutler and Detective Marsh. Still struggling, he lashed out with his foot and caught Detective Marsh a blow on the shin.

Ted will serve his sentence at Winchester Prison. If his conduct is good and he earns full remission, he will be freed when he is 66.